C000129992

Knowledge Monopolies

The Academisation of Society

Alan Shipman & Marten Shipman

SOCIETAS
essays in political
& cultural criticism

imprint-academic.com

Copyright © Alan Shipman & Marten Shipman, 2006

The moral rights of the author have been asserted.
No part of any contribution may be reproduced in any form
without permission, except for the quotation of brief passages
in criticism and discussion.

Published in the UK by Societas
Imprint Academic, PO Box 200, Exeter EX5 5YX, UK

Published in the USA by Societas
Imprint Academic, Philosophy Documentation Center
PO Box 7147, Charlottesville, VA 22906-7147, USA

ISBN 184540 028 3

A CIP catalogue record for this book is available from the
British Library and US Library of Congress

*

Marten Shipman is a retired teacher and sociologist, formerly
at the Universities of Keele, Warwick and Surrey
(Roehampton) and Director of Research and Statistics in the
Inner London Education Authority. He is the author of sev-
eral books and reports, including *The Limitations of Social
Research* (Longman).

Alan Shipman is a freelance writer and economist, formerly
at the National Institute of Economic & Social Research
andthe   Economist Intelligence Unit. His publications
include *The Market Revolution and Its Limits* (Routledge).

Contents

Introduction

Contemporary concerns over higher education are usually focused on numbers and costs. Less attention is paid to the concentration of knowledge production, validation and transmission within academia. Yet the authority of church and state, community and family has been largely replaced by the academic, profoundly altering the nature of knowledge and its impact on society. This book charts the improbable rise of the academic empire, the tactics that sustained its growth, its impact on the nature and uses of knowledge, and the likely outcome of the battle for survival caused by its spectacular growth and consequent exposure to new economic and political pressures.

The natural sciences' challenge to belief in a 4,000-year-old Earth, an orbiting sun, spontaneous generation, witchcraft, ghosts and luminiferous ether is well documented. Social sciences' equally spectacular social impact is less comfortably addressed by practising academics, since it admits the reflexivity of the enterprise: engaged researchers influencing as well as being influenced by what they study, helping to define and transform the world they set out only to reveal. Across the twentieth century the social sciences have become major parts of the curriculum in schools and higher education. They have changed our understanding of our selves, relationships and beliefs. Increasingly we think in terms of the economic, psychological and social. We assume that there is knowledge of our everyday lives together, validated by academics, reliable enough to guide policy, practice, everyday belief and behaviour. With the academisation of knowledge, social scientists need to consider the implications of their success in providing the way humans make sense of their world.

In Chapter 1 of this book we review universities' expansion as research institutions through their capture of previously independent scientific effort, and their expansion as teaching institutions through the absorption of professional accreditation. Chapter 2 outlines the ways academics acquired, on the basis of reason and research, the unconditional authority previously wielded mystically by priests or mythically by charismatic rulers; changes to the status of knowledge, and the use of peer review to reinforce its internal validation, are identified as especially important to successful academisation. Chapter 3 examines the changes to the organisation of knowledge, and of knowledge-creating activity, that have enabled the academy to multiply the scale of its research and teaching activities while strengthening its control over the process, and the authority over society that this control provides.

The reinvention of knowledge as something exclusive to the academy, and universities' ability to engender and enter 'knowledge society' without losing authority over it, rests on its ability to reconceptualise the world through models, the theme of Chapter 4. The shift from perception of ourselves and our world as something constructed, not retrieved from past records or even revealed from 'objective' observation, took previous limits off natural science and led to the creation of social science, as chronicled in Chapter 5. The occasionally advantageous, and not infrequently disastrous, impact of model-based creation and professional application of academised knowledge is examined in Chapter 6. With increasing specialisation straining their ability to control the interpretation and application of knowledge, and increasing scepticism over universities' exercise of their knowledge monopoly driving calls for tougher external regulation, Chapter 7 argues that it is more than just the shrinkage of public funding that puts today's academy under pressure to take up lessons from the business world. Chapter 8 draws conclusions on how the academy can regain the direction and dialogue endangered by its relentless specialisation, and the legitimacy lost in its imperfect transition from exclusivity to social engagement.

Chapter 1

The Omnivorous Academy

Europe pioneered the modern university, with those at Bologna, Oxford and Paris already established in the twelfth century. But by the mid-19th these ancient models were showing their age, viewed more often as roadblocks than as gateways to the industry and democracy taking shape around them. The academy's inability to promote radical new thinking, and reluctance to adopt it, had pushed other institutions to the centre of knowledge, culture and administration. Its imposition of an 'academic' curriculum was seen as frustrating upward mobility by putting a second-class stamp on technical and vocational education.

The twentieth century brought a spectacular turnaround. Universities' research eclipsed the authority of the religious, familial and traditional, and their teaching became the near-universal third stage of popular education as living standards rose. The causes and consequences of this 'academisation' of knowledge are often buried beneath problems arising from the increased numbers, as up to half of school leavers are channelled into higher education institutions still only organised and resourced for much lower proportions. These organisational problems obscure, but ultimately relate to, simultaneous changes in academia as an institution and in its production, validation and application of knowledge. Academic concepts become everyday meanings. The increasing numbers matter, but it is academia as a key but taken for granted institution that is changing our knowledge of the world and the way we make our lives meaningful.

Back from the Dead

Universities' early history, especially in their European birthplaces, makes their later marginalisation unsurprising. The academy had only ever educated a tiny minority — mostly in theologies that discouraged the search for any undiscovered truth. As late as 1950 only one UK school-leaver in twenty could expect to find a place at university. As a knowledge creator, the modern academy had emulated the medieval monastery in defending scriptures that encouraged leaps of faith, but looked askance on more reasoned acts of imagination. Early displays of free enquiry by Oxford scholars Roger Bacon (1219–94) and Thomas Hobbes (1588–1679) were soon blotted out by the valedictory smoke of those on the wrong side of the Reformation debates. Most of the pathbreaking natural science discoveries that reshaped Europe in the 16th Century were made outside universities, in private laboratories and discussion rooms. From Leonardo da Vinci (1452–1519) and Galileo Galilei (1564–1642) to Charles Darwin (1809–82) and Sigmund Freud (1856–1939), the academy proved neither a relevant location for natural enquiry nor a safe haven when it offended prevailing religious values. Its paucity of places and propensity to assign them on respectability of background rather than strength of mind ensured that most pathbreaking scholarship took place beyond its walls.

The few universities then in existence perpetuated an Aristotelian view of the world: axiomatic, static and geocentric. Escape from this framework was often easier in the guise of a royal tutor (Hobbes), a mercenary (Descartes) or a lens-grinder (Spinoza) than as a wanderer in the college gardens. In France, economics had its first stirrings in the physiocratic theories of Quesnay (1694–1774), a surgeon, and Turgot (1727–81), Louis XVI's finance minister. Both contributed to the *Encyclopedie*, published between 1751 and 1772, most of whose other illustrious contributors — including Diderot (1713–84), Rousseau (1712–78) and Voltaire (1694–1778) were dramatists, novelists, journalists, social commentators, political agitators, but noticeably not academics.

Most of today's recognisable sciences (the term slowly replaced 'natural philosophy' from around 1830) were founded outside universities. The Royal Society had been mainly a club of friends, patrons and interested gentlemen amateurs. Its efforts to make members share and publish their results were often hampered by personal or commercial rivalries, such as the long stand-off between leading mind Isaac Newton and secretary Robert Hooke; publication was more usually in magazines such as the *Quarterly Review* or the *Edinburgh Review*. The nascent 'knowledge society', diffusing its ideas so they could be deployed for practical advantage, reacted against an institution that had traditionally confined knowledge to an elite, and detached its intrinsic worth from social values or economic value.

Yet by 1950 this moribund, outmoded institution was about to enter the most sustained and spectacular growth of any social institution. By the end of the century it would dominate social thought, activity and organisation in a way no mid-century political dictator had ever achieved. In 1900 there had been 14 universities in Britain with 20,000 students. This had risen to 31 universities with 100,000 students by the time of the Robbins Report (1963), whose recommendations accelerated the growth. By the end of the century there were 176 higher education institutions, including 115 universities, enrolling over 1,300,000 full-time and 900,000 part-time undergraduate students, and employing over 70,000 full-time staff. Postgraduate intake rose proportionally even more strongly: from 43,000 full-time and 18,000 part-time higher degree students in 1970 to over 170,000 full-time and nearly 300,000 part-time at the century's end. In October 2004, the number of students arriving at UK universities exceeded 1 million for the first time.

As remarkable as the rise in numbers were the reasons for the expansion. Whereas ancient universities cloistered themselves to shut out the distractions of the world, their modern counterparts opened their doors onto main city streets, or invited the new commercial realities onto their campuses. Universities were being pressed to engage with economic and social affairs, stripping away the insulation through which academics had sought knowledge for its own sake. When London and other major towns established their first universities in the second half of the nineteenth century, they were surrounded by an array of institutions that showed the unmet demand for technical and professional skills. Colleges of Science, Dissenting Academies, Training Colleges, Technical Colleges, Mechanics and Evening Institutes, Literary, Philosophical and Statistical Societies answered to workers' and professionals' as well as industrialists' need for new knowledge, comprising a genuine public sphere. Many marched towards university status in the subsequent century.

The Robbins Report (1963) saw expansion and reform of higher education as essential for maintaining a competitive position in the world. A generation later, the Dearing Report (1997) identified the university as the key source of knowledge and human capital for underpinning prosperity and human wellbeing in a democratic society. Where higher education had once been seen, like the wider welfare state, as a luxury product of economic development, it was now widely viewed as a vital input. Its expansion was prioritised by poorer countries seeking a way into industrial development as much as by richer countries seeking a way out of it.

Feeding and Fuelling the Demand for Knowledge

In Britain, the demand for a public education service was growing by the second half of the nineteenth century. When Lowe explained the need to 'educate our masters' he was acknowledging the political imperative of reform, as legislated shortening of work hours gave ordinary people more time to think about the world they were in, and extensions of the electoral franchise gave them more incentive to do so. The state's willingness to supply education also rose as, in the second half of the nineteenth century, weaknesses in appointment and promotion by patronage were acknowledged, and institutional improvement was sought — starting with the army and civil service — through a switch to appointment on merit.

Public knowledge expansion was driven principally by public authorities, channelling taxation into education, healthcare and public infrastructure, and by churches and other voluntary-sector institutions, motivated by religious or charitable values. Both acted simultaneously on supply and demand, putting more resources into educational provision and using subsidy or sponsorship to enable people to use it. At the start of the process, few individuals had the financial resources to acquire such knowledge, and few private enterprises saw any need to help them do so. But public authorities foresaw the disabling dearth of engineers and other professionals if private enterprise continued to step up their recruitment without financing more training. This was reinforced by the public sector's own growing need for such skills to build and run the hospitals, schools, housing projects, sanitation schemes, power stations, rail, electricity and gas networks for which it had assumed responsibility.

A partial reform of the civil service in 1855 introduced competitive entry by examination. A focus on subjects mostly taught in the independent schools and ancient universities still confined recruitment to a restricted intellectual elite, but in 1870 recruitment by open competition finally replaced patronage in the civil service. The army made similar slow reforms following incompetent displays in the Crimean War (1854–56), with aristocratic purchase of commissions abolished in 1868. 'Philosophical radicals' led by Jeremy Bentham (1748–1832) had successfully battled laissez-faire to assert the need for efficient administration based on knowledge of social conditions. With the municipal public works projects of the nineteenth century, and the expansion of welfare services through the twentieth, government also stepped up its procurement of knowledge-based services on behalf of the wider society. Educational, medical, housing and transport were increasingly purchased on behalf of ordinary citizens, while companies and organisations were recipients of growing 'corporate welfare', as engineers, lawyers, accountants and other professionals were trained at public expense for private sector benefit.

As with more recent knowledge-economy breakthroughs (telephone, broadcasting, internet), the academy ensured take-up of its rising supply — of knowledge and professionals imbued with it — by enrolling government as a principal customer. Locally and nationally, the state needed new ideas and skill-holders for its own activities, especially public administration. But sustainable growth of higher education depended on public willingness to support governments that imposed the higher taxes needed to fund it, and to pay for it directly if the state ceased to do so. As they changed the conventional wisdom in existing disciplines, and launched additional ones in response to new discoveries, universities had to raise the public demand for public knowledge in step with its supply. Today, a knowledge of clinical medicine might seem essential for practice as a doctor or surgeon, and economics a useful input to a business career. But those who brought medical training into the university, and launched its first economics degrees, struggled to attract sufficient students. Patients preferred known remedies, even for new industrial-age diseases, and entrepreneurs viewed a university education more as an escape route from business than a means to run it better.

Until prospective employers recognised the value of new courses, even those who could afford to enrol in them had no financial incentive to do so. Having embraced what they believed was a formula for continuous knowledge production, universities had to ensure its continuous consumption on an equally large scale. Their triple need — for new research funds, new students and new sponsors — was solved in one by allying academisation to the century-old trend of professionalisation.

Incorporating the Professions and Training Institutions

Aware that the ancient universities had neither the capacity nor the inclination to raise enrolments to meet the new training demand, the major cities playing host to the new industrial and administrative expansion hastened to set up new ones. Most already possessed literary and philosophical institutions, historical and statistical societies, medical schools, dissenting academies and mechanics institutes. There were twenty residential teacher training colleges by

1850. Through the century a variety of institutions were established to train the new or rapidly expanding professional groups including accountants, doctors, nurses, social workers, teachers, technicians and musicians, often supported by local enterprise.

Once established, the new professional class drove reform, particularly in education and through the parliamentary Reform Bills of 1832, 1867 and 1884. Bentham was a co-founder of University College London; his cadaver still sits in its entrance hall, a riposte to earlier institutions' religious relics that has so far withstood the test of time. King's College London was established soon afterwards, to counter this godless presence in Gower Street. But Bentham's radicalism signalled a new, knowledge-based view of social improvement and political reform. Requiring information on contemporary conditions and on the likely impact of public policies to identify 'the greatest happiness of the greatest number', utilitarianism provided a calculus for optimising social action, re-basing it on facts.

The growing need to staff, and regulate, increasingly large-scale industry fuelled concern for adequate technical training. From 1832, when the Board of Trade's Statistical Department was established, a widening array of Royal Commissions, Poor Law and Civil Service Commissioners, factory inspectors, statistical and charitable societies provided data for policy analysis, and a basis for academic study. The global spread of this late nineteenth-century transformation of British society was accelerated by British Imperial imposition, and emulation in Europe and America. Even the ancient universities were forced to respond, with Cambridge establishing the Cavendish Laboratory and Oxford adopting Modern Greats (Philosophy, Politics and Economics), shortly after the 1871 Test Act had removed the remaining clerical regulations from these ancient universities.

The Samuelson Commission (1884), concerned about growing foreign competition, reported flourishing technical, science and art schools, often organised by employers and enthusiastically welcomed by employees. Most prominent were the Mechanics Institutes, whose evening classes provided practical instruction for skilled workers from the 1820s. London University's Birkbeck College, and the University of Manchester's Institute of Science and Technology, developed from such institutes, many of which achieved national reputations. But on the advice of industrialists, the Samuelson Commission dismissed theoretical studies, upholding a long tradition of keeping professional training 'practical'. This was also reflected in the professionalisation of increasingly narrow crafts, and the resultant proliferation of qualifying associations aimed at quality control. Grays Inn for lawyers had been founded in 1391, and the Worshipful Company of Spectacle Makers in 1629, but a major proliferation occurred in the century after 1850.

Qualifying associations had 625,000 full and 125,000 student members by the 1960s. But technological and legal developments, placing new demands on practitioners, soon meant that newcomers were not sufficiently prepared by age 16 or 18 for immediate entry to full-time courses for professional qualification. Higher and further education institutions stepped in to provide the necessary extra tuition, alongside colleges established by the professional associations themselves. From 1889 cities and the new county councils were able to establish colleges; central government funding was made available from 1890, initially from a tax on whisky.

Recognition of the need for a conceptual and general-knowledge base for practical skills increased with the economic pressures following WWII. The Percy Report (1945), the Barlow Report (1946) and the White Paper on Technological Education (1956) led to the establishment of Colleges of Advanced Technology (CATs) in 1960, and the movement towards the incorporation of technical and training institutions into higher education. But professions were wary of control by central or local government and their agencies. As regulators, these might be tempted to distort professional standards for political gain. As employers, they might drive down professionals' market value by making qualification easier. Professions' concern to maintain their price and prestige ensured their acceptance of absorption into educational institutions that stayed independent of the state, and were initially just as selective in their intake.

The absorption of professional training institutions underpinned academia's twentieth-century expansion, especially through the new civic universities. Medicine and law had often been part of the medieval university, with medical schools such as St. Bartholomew's active from the twelfth century. The Apothecaries Act of 1815 systematised medical training, in schools that were usually affiliated to universities or university colleges. Universities also met the increased demand for lawyers by organising their first degree courses. This set the trend for accountancy, management and marketing, with universities offering academic groundwork to degree level, before students moved on to complete their qualification as commercial trainees.

Integration of professional training, with its large, regular and publicly funded intake, secured a vital financial boost, especially for newly founded universities. For justification, the acquiring institutions pointed to a change in the nature of professional knowledge, which meant that practical skills alone were no longer enough to ensure well-paid or long-lasting employment. Academisation allowed professionals to distinguish themselves from the aristocratic amateurs of the past. Qualification required proven skill and analytical ability, which inherited wealth or family background could no longer guarantee. Training in general principles also enabled professionals to keep ahead of upwardly-mobile craft and technical workers. They were equipped to assess wider problems, decide new courses of action and acquire new skills, rather than repeating narrowly defined actions that lost effectiveness when the situation changed.

Universities promised to deliver a general professional preparation before the start of specialist on-the-job training, enabling recipients eventually to transcend their professional focus and move into the higher levels of enterprise management or politics. General capabilities, acquired and certified off the job, were a necessary complement to specific skills, and increasingly a desirable replacement for them. Academisation of the professions built on, and reinforced, the gradual extension of schooling and technical training. It fuelled a rising expectation of what such education could provide. As more people enjoyed full-time schooling for longer, more were acclimatised to higher education as the next phase. By the last quarter of the twentieth century the arts, technical, social work and teacher training institutions were an integral part of higher education.

Until the substantial rise in resourcing prompted by the Robbins Report (1963), training institutions remained under financial and time pressure to focus on skills and practice, plus some personal and moral guidance for future semi-professionals. Staff-student ratios were ungenerous, and academic content was often squeezed by the need to pack training and practice into a short certificated course. The universities, still catering for a tiny minority of school-leavers, enjoyed greater funding, study time and independence from government, and could confer more prestigious staff titles and student qualifications. Colleges of Advanced Technology were to form the apex of pyramids of technical colleges, and the Percy Report had called for them to offer degree-level courses. But a minority report by Lord Percy recommended that they should not be universities, and degree level courses were only agreed in 1956.

There was a double edge to the widespread mid-century belief in limits to growth of the universities, perhaps not far above their then enrolment of around 5% of those leaving school. A long tail of activities was assumed to be inherently 'practical', not needing an analytical dimension. The same was believed of those who came forward to train for these activities, seen as risking confusion and constrained performance if too much abstract thought were forced on them. The policymaking elite often reflected on its own academic bias — eloquence in elaborating the theory of electrical conductivity, unmatched by any ability to wire a plug — and assumed an equal and opposite practical bias on the part of the majority. Resistance to radical change in the university curriculum was long lasting. The Barlow Report (1946) had recommended a doubling of the output of scientists from the universities, but not at the expense of the arts and humanities, or of any devaluation of education to form character, temperament and wider qualities of mind.

Reluctance to alter higher education's priorities was predictable, coming from committees mainly drawn from Oxbridge, never noted for their speed of adaptation. At Oxford the study of Greek was compulsory until 1920, and some Latin remained a condition for matriculation (entry for school leavers) until 1960. Cambridge maintained similar restrictions. Women were only allowed to take degrees from 1920, being allowed into lecture halls but not into exam rooms with their male counterparts. Their full admission to degrees, and staff membership of Senate, had to wait until 1948.

Teaching the Teachers

Scepticism over whether addition of theoretical knowledge could do anything to improve practical skills or moral rectitude was most apparent in the training of teachers. The first teacher training college, Borough Road, opened in 1808. Yet even in 1900, after a century in which elementary schooling was slowly made universal, there were still twelve untrained teachers for each trained one. Only in 1833 was £20,000 granted to religious denominations for school building. Teacher training was supported by government grants from 1846, with selected students apprenticed to a schoolmaster for five years and examined by inspectors. An increasing number of successful applicants were selected for places in the training colleges, of which there were 49 by 1890. From 1902 local education authorities were also empowered to establish colleges. There were over 100 of these by 1960, with another 50 in the voluntary sector. But on the eve of prime minister Harold Wilson's 'white heat of the technological revolution', most children were still being schooled by teachers who never graduated in their subject.

The training colleges not only produced too few teachers, particularly following the 1870 Education Act, but were also criticised for training them to too low a level. The new civic universities, situated in the large towns with the most pressing shortages of trained teachers, and attracted by the grants available for student teachers, pressed for involvement in closing the gap. By 1901 they were providing a quarter of all teacher training places, and met the increased demand for graduate secondary school teachers following the 1902 Education Act. Despite continued opposition from within academia and government, day training in universities was seen as guaranteeing educated teachers at minimum cost.

As with other emerging professions, incorporation into the university meant academisation of what was taught. Within the universities Education became a major department, its junior members becoming 'reflective practitioners' while their seniors turned exclusively to analysing and conceptualising the schoolteacher's craft. Insights from history, philosophy, psychology and sociology were grafted onto the practical training, even within one year postgraduate courses. The Robbins Report (1963) recommended that training colleges be renamed Colleges of Education, conferring Bachelor of Education (BEd) degrees. The certificate courses finished with the entry of 1979, and teaching was on track to become a fully graduate profession. From 1980 colleges expanded, diversified and often amalgamated with former polytechnics, so that by 1992 most were formally part of the university sector.

Colleges' prioritisation of academic content, anticipating university status, drew frequent complaint from inspectors and teachers' unions that practical classroom skills were being neglected. Intellectual input to teacher training had wider social repercussions, probed further in Chapter 6. When colleges finally merged into universities, government imposed detailed criteria for the approval of courses through the National Council for the Accreditation of Teacher Education (NCATE), established in 1984. The academisation of social work has followed in an almost identical fashion, with other 'caring' professions taking the same track as they expand. Training moves into higher education to gain academic accreditation and prestige, as well as to ensure better general education for the practitioners. Professional associations and government thereafter worry about the cost of academisation, through neglect of practical skills and on-the-job exposure; but they cannot reverse the process, without accusations of de-skilling professionals and shortchanging clients.

Incorporating Commerce, Arts, Culture and Media

Absorption of the professions was followed by the academy's one major burst of 'internal' growth, fuelled by the social sciences (charted more fully in Chapter 5). Social sciences' spread within academia opened the way for a further wave of incorporation, centred on extensions of arts and humanities, most of which have now become subjects of study and objects of research at universities. Like the professions, these activities could gain prestige, if not practical input, from the natural and social science now pursued in the academy, which had an equally strong incentive to draw them in. Degrees from tourism and librarianship to creative writing have duly made their appearance, many enhancing the area of study by prefixing it with Business, Critical, Cultural, Economic, Gender, Human, Management, Psychological, Social or Sociological, to emphasise its new academic foundation.

Academic contributions have supplemented and often replaced the skills that dominated earlier courses of training, usually outside higher education, often in apprenticeships. Cookery was a major subject in teacher training into the 1960s. It was converted into Domestic Science and then Home Economics. One of the present authors taught the first course in the Sociology of Home Economics. Now 41 universities offer Food Science and Nutrition as a first degree, 25 a higher degree, 14 a diploma and 4 a certificate. Biology, Biotechnology, Microbiology, Chemistry, Economics and Sociology have replaced the teacher-training skill of scheduling production of a securely coiled Chelsea Bun within a school double period.

The academisation of management and marketing has been an especially significant step. Quantitatively, this has provided one of the largest areas of postwar teaching and research expansion, especially in Europe and North America. In Britain, business or management studies was by 2004 offered as a first degree in 105 universities or associated colleges, as a higher degree by 82, a diploma by 61 and a certificate by 14. Those who know what kind of management they want to be in can run down another lengthening list of prefixes from Health Services and Facilities to Hospitality and Tourism. Business schools' boost to a university's research and teaching resources is amplified by the wealth of their client group: aspiring managers' propensity to pay large MBA course fees, and companies' keenness to sponsor research and continuing education for their executives, ensures a cashflow that can quickly overtake that of longer-established faculties. Poaching their subject matter from history, organisation theory, game and decision theory, statistics, engineering, economics and other social sciences, business -schools often do the same with their staff and students, who are lured by clearer career paths and better financial support.

Qualitatively, management can — along with computer science — be regarded as one of the first professions that universities have created, and not just incorporated. Although synthesised (like all 'Studies' subjects) from a range of older-established disciplines, business and management have now acquired their distinct methodologies (case studies, simulations, opinion surveys and text-mining ranking high), their own set of 'classic' texts, and refereed journals read exclusively within the profession. By mid-century in America, and end-century in Europe, management scientists had achieved a professional distinction from management practitioners, more extreme even than that of academic lawyers and physicians. Business scholars are now numerous enough to form their own internal market, exchanging ideas among themselves without the necessity to take input from, or target their output at, the commercial world outside. Their discipline has acquired the specialist jargon, models and statistics needed to exclude ordinary managers from the discussion, which can now treat firms and their leaders as objects of study not expected to answer back.

A generation of business professors who practised before they preached has been replaced by one whose academic management training was never needlessly interrupted by spells behind the executive desk. Journals once aimed at practitioners now feature subjects that sidestep their agenda, couched in terms that defy their vocabulary — a sure sign of success in escaping the perilous business environment for the faster-growing, more cyclically resilient academic one. Business has repeated the success of English literature, musicology, media studies and (in the UK) accountancy: subjects that grow much bigger, and enjoy more stable markets, than the real-world activities that inspired them. Other new disciplines can expect to join them as more, like Moliere's Monsieur Jourdain, discover they are speaking prose, and fall silent while they seek to formalise its rules.

Conclusion: The Virtuous Circle

Universities expanded because they had become important, economically and socially. The governments, of all political stripes, that committed themselves to expensive programmes of building new universities and funding more students and academics to staff them, believed they were laying foundations for a stronger economy and a more just and contented society. But it can equally be said that universities became important because they expanded. Having prodded the state into initially enlarging them, they entered a phase of self-sustaining growth, not open to derailment even when government support began to recede.

Increased participation in schooling, eventually compulsory to age 16, boosted the number qualified to enter higher education. The incentive to do so came from a comparison of graduate and non-graduate earnings that suggested a big lifetime return on the degree-course investment. Academic credentials became ever more necessary to pass employers' screening procedures, even if not relevant to performance of the actual work. The rate of return on higher education 'investment' thus stabilised or even rose, despite its graduates being channelled into tasks for which they were previously overqualified. A situation was created in which students, their families and prospective employers regarded university study as worth obtaining even if the costs are not met by the state. Degrees were now needed to obtain interesting, well-paid employment as well as post-school social initiation.

Social hierarchy has been reordered, with efficiency and apparent equity, on the basis of paper qualifications. When every applicant had good school-leaving grades, a first degree marked out the genuinely able ones; when everyone had a first degree, the master's became the distinction. Thus the twentieth century in Britain started with the completion of elementary schooling for all and ended with a target of half each age group entering higher education. Expectations of a university education had spread across the sexes, social classes and ethnic minorities. By 2000, women outnumbered men among full and part-time undergraduates and postgraduates.

The growth of compulsory education is, by definition, supply-driven. Governments lengthen and widen free school provision because they judge it to be in the individual and social interest, even if recipients do not always see it that way. In contrast, universities offer 'post-compulsory' education whose growth depended on demand — for places on its courses and outputs from its research. For almost a century after their late nineteenth-century revival, universities relied on governments to furnish the increased demand, by paying the fees and maintenance of an increasing number of students, and channelling substantial public funds into research. But by the end of the twentieth century, demand for universities' services had been extensively re-privatised, without curbing their expansion. The centrality created by that injection of public funds had created an expansionary momentum that can now survive their inexorable withdrawal. A major institution disseminating knowledge and accrediting knowers has been established.

Chapter 2

The Interpretive Elite

The modern university creates new knowledge through research, refinement and recombination of existing ideas, and validates the knowledge claims made by others. It consolidates knowledge into disciplines that define courses of study and guide research activities. It disseminates knowledge to its own students, the wider research community and society in general, accrediting those judged successful. It also regulates applications of knowledge beyond its grey or redbrick walls, in ways the next chapter investigates further. By uniquely securing these functions, universities have become the chief architects and beneficiaries of the 'knowledge society'. Their rise (or revival) is linked to the movement of knowledge into the centre of private and professional activity, and of public policy and debate.

Because of their initial subordination to church and state, and wariness of confrontation with them, universities took time to recognise and rally behind the quest for 'scientific' knowledge. Those who studied and taught at them did so within strictly defined religious boundaries. The quest to challenge faith with reason took place mainly outside the ivory towers. From Galileo in the sixteenth century to Darwin in the late nineteenth and Einstein in the early twentieth, many of the key natural and social science breakthroughs were the work of men with independent means, as well as minds.

Making Knowledge a 'Public Good'

The fear of religious retribution, and the need to profit from any exploitable discoveries, prevented the open dissemination of knowledge for which universities stood. Leonardo da Vinci (1452–1519) mirror-wrote his notes, and published nothing of his experiments in his lifetime. Copernicus (1473–1543) waited until near death before publication he knew might hasten it. Astronomer-royal John Flamsteed fought for years to stop Isaac Newton obtaining his observational data. Science was pursued in private, in secret societies or the libraries of the powerful. Even when they worked in a public institution by day, those with the new ideas usually postponed their discussion for closed-door debate after night fell.

To make more systematic progress, however, thinkers needed to pool their efforts and check one another's work. Scholarship demanded community: for protection against religious or political attack, dialogue to avoid duplication, and authentication of results, once these moved beyond common comprehension and commonsense. But to become centres for the new thinking, and make increasing claims on social resources while challenging cherished social beliefs, universities first had to show that 'scientific' knowledge creation outperformed the previous methods, or carried a justification in itself.

In England, public recognition of the legitimacy of scientific thinking arrived with the Royal Society, founded in 1660 and granted a Royal Charter by Charles II in 1662. The Society first met in Gresham College, established by Tudor financier Thomas Gresham (1519–79). Gresham's patronage and wealth ensured security for its meetings, although religion and politics were excluded from discussion. Five of the Society's twelve founders held professorships at the College and at Oxford. But many of the founders were adherents of Freemasonry, Rosicrucians, Illuminati, and other secret societies promoting cooperative development of knowledge outside the university system. The French Academy of Sciences was established two years later in Paris, with a similar founding membership, again under royal patronage.

Experimentation at this time — even in alchemy — was mainly small-scale and laboratory-based, used to test general hypotheses inspired by abstract theories. But industrialisation opened a new phase of technology-driven, workshop-based experiment, to try out specific ideas in answer to practical problems. Scientists like Pasteur and Joule worked to government or private industry commissions, while those like Edison and Watt sought to fund their work through its entrepreneurial reward.

Recognising wealth creation (and consequent national imperial and military power) as a new justification for science, the Royal Institution was founded in 1799 for 'the promotion, extension and diffusion of Science and of Useful Knowledge'. It became the intellectual home of Michael Faraday (1791–1867), who with James Clerk Maxwell (1831–79) tackled many of the mysteries of chemistry and physics highlighted by technological development in the centuries after Newton. By the end of the nineteenth century both public and private sectors were seen to need professional expertise.

Established professions from medicine to military command were becoming 'evidence based', and new professions were emerging from systematic investigation and analysis in such areas as finance, accounting, engineering, administration and town planning. Fears of how new microscopes and telescopes might filter the Light of the World led the Vatican to affirm Papal infallibility in 1870. But elsewhere in Europe and America, science (natural and social) was being incorporated into university curricula, with applications appearing alongside — and often forcing revisions to — the age-old assertions of principle.

People with relevant skills and ideas were increasingly seen to be the basis of prosperity and wellbeing. But the new name for knowledge that enhanced personal productivity and income — Human Capital — reflected industrialism's focus on private profit as the way to social improvement. Professionals could expect good monetary rewards, not only by controlling the supply of their skills, but also by augmenting the demand. They did so by extending the range of financial, industrial, social and personal problems their expertise could claim to solve; and by persuading governments to intervene to promote and control the use of such solutions, and accreditation of the necessary experts. Passage of the relevant regulations was helped by professionals' growing parliamentary and committee representation as politics, too, became a profession.

Absorbing the professions had given universities a new source of research objectives and funds, as well as of training opportunities, as professionals sought more analytical approaches to their previously practical vocation. By the late nineteenth century, public intellectuals like historian Thomas Carlyle (1795–1881) and Thomas Huxley (1825–95), with reputations built on private research and public speaking, were recognising universities' growing prestige by seeking professorships in them. Systematic investigation and calculation promised to enhance, if not supplant, the intuitions, inspired guesses and random stabs that had previously guided much enquiry. This was encouraged by the shift from scripture-based to evidence-based practice that universities were bringing to other areas of knowledge. The natural sciences absorbed by European and American universities had, from the late nineteenth century, changed the way the world was understood, as physicists and chemists in Newton's wake exposed the intricacy of the world's design, and biologists in Darwin's wake undermined belief in a divine designer. Study of the human in society wrought comparable changes in a different way, on a very different world.

Objectifying Knowledge

Enlightenment scholars believed they were rooting out myth and superstition, replacing them with fact and reasoned opinion. They were also breaking free of the constraining belief that knowledge was finite, with history's course predetermined by an agency that already possessed all the knowledge, or a causal sequence that inexorably unfolded. Their vision was of knowledge and its applications being infinitely extendable, and humanity enjoying an open-ended future guided by its pursuit. Even when regularities were discovered or developmental laws proclaimed, the intention was to help societies change their direction, not fatalistically accept it.

Pioneers of the natural sciences envisaged a move from *retrieved* to *revealed* knowledge. Pearls of wisdom from ancient scriptures or archives, once assumed to be correct, were now to be treated as mere hypotheses to be tested against real-world events. Hypotheses' truth or falsity could be established inductively by observation and experiment, or deductively from axioms, greatly accelerating the rate at which new ideas could gain acceptance.

Practitioners of 'Enlightenment' arts and humanities pursued a parallel move from *retrieved* to *constructed* knowledge. Escaping a traditional repertoire of themes and techniques, they felt free to turn existing art forms in new directions, and to harness new technological developments for artistic expression. The new ways to represent traditional subjects that characterised Europe's Renaissance were followed by a Reformation search for new subjects to represent, and an industrialisation phase in which novels, photography, cinema, broadcasting, recorded music, electric instruments, audiovisual and interactive media emerged as new sources of art and culture, alongside the traditional staples of theatre, live music and visual art. Cultural knowledge matched scientific output in appearing infinitely expandable, with the added feature that old media and messages need not be superseded by new ones. For every critic who declares an artistic or cultural form to be outmoded, there is another working on its revival, and revealing a vibrant 'retro' clientele.

Social sciences, arriving after natural science and humanities had taken these two divergent paths, swayed between the two and eventually alighted on an intermediate stance. The founders, convinced that more could be revealed about the human condition than 'humanities' had so far achieved, hoped to emulate the method of the natural sciences. While pushing social sciences in the direction of revealed truth, they also dragged the natural sciences in the direction of constructed truth. Theoretical assessment of science showed there would always be propositions whose truth was not deducible from the most exhaustive set of axioms, and not inducible from the most exhaustive data set. Quantum theory exposed aspects of natural reality that might, like social reality, be changed by the act of observation. Social Studies of Science showed that received wisdoms, personal preferences and instinctive beliefs could shape scientists' preferred view of the world, often making these the cause rather than the consequence of the empirical tests put forward as upholding them. Postmodernism challenged the whole notion of organisms stepping outside the natural and social worlds they were a part of, sufficiently far to observe or interpret them with any objectivity.

Under this onslaught even as staunch an admirer as Karl Popper, recognising the impossibility of inductive 'proof', argued that natural science could only be certain over what could *not* count as knowledge, any positive beliefs being strictly provisional. Historical and social studies of science went further in this 'subjectivisation', highlighting the extent to which people (including experts) arrive at beliefs before they find empirical support and retain them after empirical refutation. The power of models and pressure of peers can shape scientists' belief (and disbelief) at least as powerfully as laboratory observations and test results. So the conceptual trend has moved inexorably from *The Social Construction of Reality* (by sociologists Peter Berger and Thomas Luckmann) via *The Construction of Social Reality* (by philosopher John Searle) to *The Reality of Social Construction* — not in need of an author, because it's already widely taken as read.

The Interpretive Shift

In most areas of natural science, theories can still be observationally or experimentally tested. Misleading representations or inaccurate predictions can cast doubt on inappropriate ideas, even if no rejection ever proves decisive. But even if scientific theory stays largely 'objective', its application is a social process, becoming more so as science becomes an increasingly collective, collaborative venture in university and industrial settings. This is recognised in a change in the conventional distinction between science and technology, from one based on the type of activity to one based on where and why it takes place. Science is pursued in an 'academic' setting with rewards based on recognition and accreditation; technology is pursued in a 'commercial' setting primarily for financial reward. Scientists build reputation by proclaiming knowledge publicly, technologists build fortunes by exploiting it privately (Dasgupta & David 1994, Whitley 2000). The comfortable implication was that 'pure' researchers would not object to others profiting from their brain waves, if adequately plied with prizes and professorships. But the distinction may be fading, as companies encourage their scientists to engage in 'blue skies thinking' while academic scientists take on commercial projects, as universities push the exploitation of their intellectual property rights.

The absence of clear criteria for what counts as valid knowledge, in terms either of the results produced or the people and processes producing them, calls for another route to knowledge validation. Academic refereeing and referencing have provided this, thereby cementing universities' new role. The preferability of models, priority of hypotheses, and tenability of theories become a matter of expert judgement, when there is no better way to show which best fit the world. The information-age academy takes over this gate-keeping role.

Reconceptualising knowledge as constructed, rather than revealed or retrieved, is a radical epistemological shift. It turns universities into an environment where academics can produce new knowledge without fear, identify new problems and prepare professionals to solve them. Constructed knowledge also presents higher education with an economic challenge: to ensure that knowledge is demanded in the greatly increased quantity in which it can now be supplied. Establishing the social centrality of academically authorised knowledge and accredited professionals enabled universities to furnish such demand, and induce the public (or their governments) to pay for it.

Subjects created in the 'classical' phase of social sciences were given names that reflected their natural-science inspirations and aspirations. Economics likened itself to physics, sociology and psychology to biology, and politics to both with its analogies of organic realms and mechanics of power. In contrast, the past half-century's proliferation has relied on abandonment of these unifying perspectives, swapping scientific suffixes for more multi-faceted 'studies'. The terminology of (among others) management, media, cultural, international, translation or development studies immediately invokes a plurality of viewpoints, many possible viewpoints on the same phenomenon. The Studies' eclectic trawling of older-established disciplines gives a formula for their rapid creation, academic validation and popularisation.

Expanding Knowledge Through Specialisation

Knowledge multiplies by dividing. Academic output can be expanded through the division of labour, as dramatically as in any other production activity. Even the advance of specialisation to the point where experts within the same subject cannot easily communicate can still be defended by pointing to the productivity gains from the concentration on a precisely defined area of competence. The inexorability of specialisation and separate organisation had already forced those in charge of the biggest universities to admit their transition to spatially- and subject-divided 'multiversities', more than forty years ago. In the UK, higher education began to impose specialisation on secondary education after the 1902 Education Act. Secondary schools' subject-based curriculum was determined by university examination boards, and as late as 1945 university lecturers were marking examinations by both 16- and 18-year olds. This arrangement enabled the universities to lock-in early specialisation, and ensure smooth transition into their conventional academic disciplines.

Academic specialisation is usually explained by reference to the impossibility of any one person being expert in more than one branch of natural or social science, arts or humanities, the width of the branch getting narrower as its length extends. The time needed to assimilate existing knowledge, and the focus needed to add more, bind its advance to 'knowing more and more about less and less.' But specialisation is also fuelled by opportunities opened up by knowledge accumulation; it reflects the workings of the acquisitive as well as the inquisitive human mind. The growth areas are often around or across the borders of conventional subjects or in their applications. As new specialist communities form they move to independence, with their own titles, hierarchy, publications, international networks and research agendas.

Higher education's expansion in the second half of the twentieth century meant rapid promotion for those who adopted a fashionable specialism. As training was moved into universities, applications — particularly of social sciences — were built into professional courses. The Sociology of Education revolutionised teacher training in the 1960s as well as securing rapid promotion for those early in the field. Publishers were eager for copy; academic posts proliferated faster than the numbers qualified to fill them. The motivation to create new knowledge inevitably tangles with career ambition. A steady career path offsets the uncertainties which otherwise taint the excitement of probing unknown areas. Increasing specialisation ensured an orderly competition for the new posts opened up by academic expansion. The price was paid by the frustration of those whose promotion was blocked by the bulge of tenured young professors when growth was slowed, by limits on public budgets and loss of trust in what the new subjects could deliver.

The specialism is now the basic unit for academic research and teaching. This is a remarkable departure from earlier visions. Adam Smith (1723–90) saw himself producing a general science of society. His contemporaries at Oxford still followed a broad undergraduate curriculum, assumed to be an essential grounding for whatever profession or further study they subsequently took up. Sully (1843–1923) founded the Psychology of Childhood in Britain, but also wrote on anthropology and sociology. Herbert Simon (1916–2001), arguably the last university-tolerated polymath, was a Nobel prizewinner in economics, a pioneer of cognitive, administrative and computer sciences, and a major influence on current strands of management studies, psychology and artificial intelligence through his concept of bounded rationality. Today such involvement in all trades would likely be interpreted as mastery of none. Pioneer generalists now tend to find themselves either distilled uncomfortably into one discipline (Pareto as economist, Weber as sociologist, Galton as psychologist), or impatiently passed over by them all.

The irresistible force of specialisation in research meets the immutable object of generality in teaching. New knowledge must be traced down ever narrower seams, as witnessed by the narrowing of article and thesis titles, from explorations of general principles to the perturbations of electron orbits in the helium atom or repetitive strains of a cashier's fourth metatarsals. But it must then be joined up to give an increasingly broad education to a widening student intake. The solution most commonly pursued has been to promote 'multidisciplinary' input to courses; but parading a succession of specialists before the same students rarely satisfied either side. The University of Keele, established in 1949 with a multidisciplinary foundation year and tutorial groups bridging faculties, has since reverted to the conventional pattern. UK Research Councils fund programmes designed to promote cooperation across specialisms, and diversity in research training. But their output is more often a confusion of contributions from different specialisms than an interdisciplinary fusion of their subject matter and methods.

Private industries have proved adept at linking minds across subject boundaries for such hybrid innovations as the electronically controlled dual-fuel car, online art encyclopedia or laser-guided missile. In contrast to this commercial impulse for knocking heads together, academics' incentive is to keep them in separate clouds. Intellectual defences can be quick to shoot down any reconnaissance team that climbs out of one silo to look down the next.

Specialism's downward diffusion has proved irresistible, with more and earlier specialisation, even in traditionally general courses. A frequently cited reason is the relentless accumulation of knowledge in each subject. As each subject branch grows steadily longer, and harder to follow as it nears the cutting edge, fewer can be travelled down in a course of fixed length. But relentless flows of new knowledge do not automatically enlarge the stock. They may even cause it to shrink. Intellectual capital depreciates like any other type; and the faster arrival of ideas can speed the obsolescence of those already in place. Major breakthroughs of discovery or reasoning generally destroy more knowledge than they create. Chemistry's archives shrank substantially when it overthrew the extensive theory based on phlogiston emissions. The process is ongoing in Econometrics, as it disowns the many past papers that fall short of latest refinements in its statistical method. A preference for parsimonious explanation, and shift of emphasis from confirmation to refutation, ensures that subjects' advance often leaves them knowing less than before.

To this temporal contraction can be added a spatial contraction of knowledge, as those who still command an overview reveal how essentially consonant ideas have maintained a separate existence behind subject boundaries. The degree of shrinkage and graspability of what remains, when false distinctions and duplications are cut away, explains why toleration of grand theory declines in direct proportion to its destructive power.

Peer Review and the Mechanics of Control

The proliferation of specialisms has complicated procedures for retrieval and validation of knowledge which were originally devised for a narrow range of classical and religious texts, by monastically disciplined priests. While few remain cloistered, celibate or other-worldly, and most end their religious devotion with High Table grace, academics still view agreement among peers as the basis of validation. They now seek to inform and influence the behaviour of individuals, organisations, companies and governments far more extensively than old priesthoods hoped or dared. At the core of this enterprise is the public display of procedures and results, to enable peers to judge their reliability and relevance.

Specialisation gathers momentum as academics are assessed on their publications. Journals proliferate, not just because knowledge differentiates, but because each publication assists the production of critiques, elaborations, new directions and applications. Around 1,000 specialist social science journals are published in the US, varying from the prestigious and refereed to those circulated in-house. Escalating numbers of theses and dissertations create a nightmare for librarians. It long ago became impossible to track all relevant new material without searchable databases, or absorb it all without journals that abstract, condense and review other journals' contents. The peer-validated canon establishes the authority of academic authors, and denies legitimacy to criticisms by outsiders.

Peer review is presented as making academic life relentlessly critical, keeping researchers on their toes even as they teeter at the subject's cutting edge. Specialisation might, at the extreme, result in every practitioner monopolising their own researching and teaching niche, with no others able or willing to challenge or check their results. Peer review prevents such dangerous isolation, ensuring that academics are monitored along the way by colleagues and supervisors, and checked at the end by critical audiences and anonymous referees. Academics, and those aspiring to join them, are socialised by peer examination, grading and continuous assessment.

But peer review also offers a protective mechanism, shielding specialisms against external attack — from other specialisms, and from knowledge claims arising outside academia. The higher the level to which a particular line of reasoning is pursued, the more must assessment of its validity be left to the handful of experts who are working at comparable heights. Their limited number, and mutual familiarity gained by sharing of knowledge or conference rooms, are substantial departures from normal competitive conditions. Natural scientists seek valid knowledge through precise hypothesis and replicable investigative method. Results are open to confirmation or falsification — but only by those sufficiently informed and experienced to carry these out rigorously. Social scientists have more limited possibilities for experiment or replication, and greater scope for investigators to alter reality in the act of observing it. But this only serves to increase the importance of agreement among peers to establish validity.

Since assessing others' work takes time and energy from their own, and is unpaid and often anonymous, academics seek to limit their reviewing commitment by reviewing only 'serious' work from qualified authors at recognised institutions. Rewards are obtained by getting an early glimpse of work which, if worthwhile, can help the reviewer stay updated for their own. In principle, rigorous review of research results lessens the importance of the affiliation and credentials of those doing it. In practice, their importance is increased. Many subjects have encountered an 'approbatory spiral' in which prestigious university affiliation assists publication in top journals which then reinforces the university's prestige; for example, 50 top business schools accounted for 70% of the contents of top management journals at the turn of the century (Tischmann et al., 2000). The peer group must be joined, by proving suitability to be ranked among them, before its two-way privileges can be enjoyed.

When London's University and King's Colleges were established in the 1830s, the founders were familiar with the laxity in Oxford in particular, and did not trust lecturers to control examinations. Dons often had little experience of classified degrees, most 'Oxbridge' students emerging with a pass. The new universities, needing to achieve public confidence, submitted to external examination as the price for allowing lecturers to grade their own students. This acceptance of an independent check on internal assessment opened the door to the subsequent widening of external monitoring — to cover research and teaching quality at university, departmental and even individual level.

By making the case that their work is too abstruse to be judged by unqualified outsiders, academics have retained far greater autonomy than most of the other professions now succumbing to external regulation. Control moves beyond the autonomous institution, but stays within like-minded groups at other institutions, extending rather than eclipsing peer review. The assessment of colleges for university status, of courses, research, appointments, promotions, funding applications, examinations and theses for degrees is placed in the hands of colleagues chosen for their relevant experience and reputation.

The growing construction of academic knowledge can be seen in the increasing length of journal articles' reference sections across each decade of the second half of the twentieth century. Similarly, a social science textbook was likely to have under a hundred references in the 1960s, many hundreds forty years later. Most of these are now references to sources that are themselves referenced to others, the chain running back to Smith or Marx, Freud or Durkheim. Reference to these now-unquestioned founders confers legitimacy — a different purpose from that originally intended for referencing, which was simply to give the source of quoted information or opinion. With layered referencing, knowledge hot off the press can be safely based on work previously approved for publication.

As specialist knowledge becomes validated by peers, criticism by outsiders loses its legitimacy. The perception that academia now concentrates the best informed experts, and empowers them to assess one another's work, underlies its centrality to contemporary knowledge production. University postholders routinely curse the administrative and ceremonial duties that deflect their creative energy and drain their research time. But this sacrifice is their membership of an inner circle, confirming that their work received recognition and enabling them to give this to others. Independent scholars may have more time to think and more freedom to speak, but exclusion from the peer group means there is no guarantee that anyone will listen to what they say, or keep them informed of what others have been doing.

Small Worlds, Big Consequences

Enshrinement of peer review has enabled academic work to stay enclosed in guild-like, collegiate, self-governing and exclusive institutions. The old religious tests and celibacy rules may have gone, but the titles, rituals, obsession with quality and purity of belief, and hierarchical peer networking — often across national boundaries — remain. The authority of peer review, regarding what constitutes knowledge and its proper application, underpins academics' dual claim on knowledge society: to be central to it, and to enjoy continued autonomy from it. Two of the past century's intellectual giants concur:

> We term information scientific if and only if an uncompelled and permanent consensus can be obtained with regard to its validity (Habermas, 1972).

> In science men collaborate not because they are forced by superior authority or because they blindly follow some chosen leader, but because they realise that only in this willing collaboration can each man find his goal. Not orders, but advice determines action. Each man knows that only by advice, honestly and disinterestedly given, can his work succeed . . . (Bernal, 1939).

Bernal spoke for natural sciences, in which formulation and testing of new ideas is often a collective effort. Habermas underlines how validation of social science ideas is collective, even if lone individuals create them. The confidence in informed consensus assumes that evidence will be fully disclosed and dispassionately scrutinised. Because the mechanics of consultation are trusted, only the conclusions need be made public.

Widespread use of peer review means that the same names appear frequently as external examiners, referees, editors and members of important committees. In a narrow specialism, external and internal reviewers get to know one another, and often exchange roles. New knowledge claims are mainly judged in relation to knowledge already validated by other academics. This can easily become a closed, exclusive arrangement. It is geared to incremental additions and alterations to knowledge. The easiest path to tenure and status is to work within an established tradition, publishing in mainstream journals and referring to existing work. More substantial reconstructions, demolishing and replacing as well as extending, are usually accepted only after years of lonely battle against the consensus, often by outsiders from another discipline or in response to developments beyond the academy.

In a small specialism, being recognised as productive (hence publishable and promotable) can mean pleasing one or two of the august. The first among peers can reject submissions and delay responses, giving no reason for their decisions, sometimes not even putting these on record. Senior academics' contact remains frequently informal, across coffee tables as much as committee rooms, even as it grows increasingly international. Theirs is possibly the only world in which intellectual merit eclipses social skills as the basis for successful networking, as confirmed by the star-studded membership rolls and frequently toe-curling later life roles of the Cambridge (UK) Apostles, and fraternities of Cambridge MA.

The conservatism of consensus is well understood by students of business, who long ago observed that radical innovation almost always comes from newcomers to an industry or marginal players within it. Those that have thrived on, and invested in, the familiar product or process have little incentive to seize on a new one. Their usual response to a competitor offering a radically different approach is to eliminate it, differentiate from it or (if neither tactic works) imitate it. Privacy in peer review can build-in bias, suppress new ideas, conceal incompetence and delay decisions. Its long pedigree and wide application — to refereeing, examining, appointing, promoting and assessing funding applications — does not overcome its conflict with the basic requirement of a science to be open and public. While anonymity makes it difficult to research, flaws have been revealed by studies that seek new verdicts on already-published articles (eg Peters and Ceci in Harnad, 1982), or compare verdicts on the same paper submitted under names of different seniority, and quiz unsuccessful grant applicants (eg Wood, Meek and Harman, 1992). In one case, legal action was used to break the privacy of peer review, and possible judgemental biases were revealed (Wenneras and Wold, 1997).

Peters and Ceci sent twelve articles previously published in prestigious and refereed Psychology journals to another 38 editors and reviewers, 18–32 months after first publication, using fictitious author names. In three cases the deception was detected. In only one of the nine remaining cases was there a positive review leading to acceptance for publication. A change in author names, referees or editorial fashion — to which the system should be immune — had made papers publishable in one year unpublishable the next. While questioning the ethics of the research and insisting it could not happen in their subject, academics invited to comment on the results generally agreed that the assessment biases were clear and intolerable. The reviewing of papers without identifying their authors has since become more common, but there has been no move to end examiner anonymity.

Wenneras and Wold (1997) analysed peer-reviewer scores on applications for postdoctoral fellowships in 1995, after Sweden's Administrative Court of Appeal forced its Medical Research Council to release these. Out of 144 applicants, sixteen men and four women were successful. Statistical treatment of scores on the six criteria used showed that scientific productivity was one of only three key factors in shaping the selection. Women assessed to be as productive as men were given lower scores, and affiliation with the reviewer worked in candidates' favour. Privacy had enabled sexism and nepotism to enter 'scientific' judgement, with an important bearing on who can establish a career and what research and peer assessments they themselves go on to produce.

Among several other well-documented problems, peer reviewers show very low rates of agreement on the same paper's merits, even if they agree strongly on the rating criteria; tend to rate papers' methodologies more highly if these produce results that they agree with; favour papers that reference already-accepted articles by the same author; and discriminate against studies that present negative results (Starbuck 2003).

The realisation of potential flaws in peer review has led to many attempts to secure greater openness and clarity of procedure. In the UK, external quality checks are offered by the Academic Audit Unit of the Committee of Vice-Chancellors and Principals, and by the Higher Education Quality Council. The Dearing Report (1997) suggested improvement through the use of pre-specified criteria, standard questions to guide assessment, distribution of comments to grant applicants, and selection of 'peers' from approved lists. The

Economic and Social Research Council has established a College of Assessors to review grant applications. The Quality Assurance Agency has examined procedures for examining students, threatening refusal of accreditation if there were problems. But academics' successful defence of autonomy ensures that they staff the relevant committees, and retain control of the process. Only peers can put peer review under review. It remains central to academic quality assurance, while simultaneously insulating academia from the accountability to which all other state-supported professions must now yield.

This is a problem at the centre of academia. The further a particular line of reasoning is pursued, the more must the assessment of its validity be left to the handful of specialists who have pursued it to similar length. Academics are committed through long preparation, frequent examination and above all continuous scrutiny by established experts in specialist areas. Career prospects depend on winning approval. That investment privileges them to work among peers in institutions organised to promote the production, validation and transmission of knowledge. It confers protection and suggests that academic life is relentlessly critical, keeping researchers on their toes even as they teeter at the subject's cutting edge. At the extreme, it could result in every practitioner monopolising their own researching and teaching niche, with no-one else able or willing to check and challenge their results.

Creating the New Priesthood

Academics have achieved their present eminence by replacing previous sources of knowledge creation and validation. Chief among these were churches and political authorities. The two were often linked, with established religions securing political influence in return for conferring 'divine rights' of emperors and kings. Churches retain a strong hold on many countries' school education, especially where willing to finance it. Governments periodically try using their hold on universities' purse-strings to influence their teaching and research agenda, or at least to close the institutions and sack the academics that prove too subversive. But universities' perceived economic and social importance has forced these older power bases to cede knowledge-creating authority to them, even if it means religion and politics shrinking to minor items on a much expanded curriculum.

Monks' and priests' authority came from their literacy, backed by an authoritative church and knowledge retrieved from ancient texts. Many universities grew out of religious institutions, and most initially coexisted with them. Challenging priestly authority was a hazardous step, 'objective' explanation sometimes proving fatally objectionable to religious leaders and their followers, as Galileo and various Renaissance heretics discovered. Even when not unduly fearful of persecution, most early scientists inherited an ecclesiastical mindset, and were trying to reconcile their theory and observation with religious or mystical beliefs. When Newton went to Cambridge in 1661, the curriculum was little changed from the thirteenth century. Into the nineteenth, English universities asked students to swear to follow the 39 Articles of the Anglican Church, whose monopoly was finally broken in 1871.

Early science was often alchemy, aimed at producing gold from base metals and mixing an elixir of life. It was science mixed with magic, necessitating secrecy from competitors or spies. Many practitioners saw it as uncovering rather than undermining God's mysteries. But while fear of the heresy charge only subsided with the rejection of religious dogma in the nineteenth century, the spirit of enquiry steadily rolled back the spectre of inquisition, encouraging a challenge to the core of scholastic views of the material world. From the mid-fifteenth century, printing facilitated the circulation of texts from Protestant countries in northern Europe, and of Arab learning brought in from the south. Initially suspicious, European universities embraced accretion of knowledge through human enquiry, and by the twentieth century had become mostly secular and increasingly scientific institutions. They became an increasingly secure base for producing, validating and applying new ideas and evidence, and critically re-examining the legitimacy of traditional beliefs. By assigning pay and status based on scholarly reputation, regardless of the economic value of discoveries, the academy also shielded enquiry from co-optation by the private industry which expanded alongside it as religious rules and attitudes relaxed.

But there is more than material continuity between the priestly robe and contemporary academic dress. While knowledge may be reached by a different route, there is little change in the respect its producers expect to be accorded for it, or in their favoured methods of presentation. Utopian visions, laws, stage theories of development and predictions remain enduringly popular. From Francis Bacon's sixteenth-century *New Atlantis* to Aldous Huxley's twentieth century *Brave New World*, and from Auguste Comte's law of three stages to Herbert Spencer's supreme law of evolution and dissolution, expressions of confidence in science have been tinged with fear of possible consequences. These require its submission to expert interpretation and control, just as religious truths were judged to be dangerous unless decoded and contextualised from the pulpit. Thus in Comte's Positive stage of human development, with sociologists at its core, social regeneration would be supervised by a committee of eight French, seven English, six Germans, five Italians and four Spaniards meeting in Paris. Like any revolutionaries, those winning the battle of reason could not escape the temptation to occupy the palace from which the old guard had been chased.

Resisting Democratisation

There is a tension in simultaneously claiming engagement and exclusivity, application and detachment. Universities won access to substantial public subsidy on the basis that their outputs — authenticated knowledge and accredited individuals — promote cohesion and prosperity in the society around them. So scholars who once accumulated and archived knowledge solely for their own use come under pressure to make it popular and useful. They are forced to do so once material survival rests on attracting larger intakes onto their courses and grants for their research. Amassing knowledge for its own sake must be supplemented, if not supplanted, by pursuit of its applications for all-round benefit. 'The central task of the university in the twenty-first century is to become a key actor in the public sphere and thereby enhance the democratisation of knowledge' (Delanty, 2001: 9).

But industrial economies can achieve prolonged growth without diffusing the ownership of commercial capital, and knowledge society can expand just as far without diffusing intellectual capital. While an increasing proportion can obtain first degrees, the elite stays ahead by amassing higher degrees, and their research widens the gap between expert and lay understanding. Most 'knowledge workers' have no more ownership of the knowledge they process and apply than do skilled industrial workers over the machinery they operate. Far from sharing it out, 'knowledge society' develops by formalising and concentrating knowledge and ideas that were once widely held and discussed. Intellectualisation echoes the process by which industrialisation concentrated technology and skills previously dispersed across small, independent producers.

The tension between democratisation and academisation is highlighted by angry reactions to the growing pressure for regulation and accountability in higher education. Democracy uses average opinion to set rules for individual and collective action, when compromise is needed in the absence of right or wrong answers. Academia devises rules by identifying right or wrong answers, putting expert consensus above average opinion. Whereas political authority is strengthened by a democratic mandate, academic authority is eroded if subjected to public approval. The natural world is assumed to exist independently of its observers and their preferences. The social world is formed and transformed by its members in ways they may not be able to observe or neutrally assess. To invite public discussion of what counts as knowledge, and how it should be taught, would be to subordinate fact to value and reasoned to wishful thinking.

Just as priestly and military rulers have in the past only answered to clerical or martial courts, academics reserve the right to be judged solely by their peers. Committees and referees appointed by external authority are viewed as lacking the necessary insight and objectivity, even if their members are drawn mainly from the academic world. Presenting loss of trust in experts' authority as an effect rather than the cause of recent challenges to their autonomy, a leading philosopher views efforts to regulate her own and other professions as betraying outsiders' inability to grasp what they do. 'Each profession has its proper aim, and this aim is not reducible to meeting set targets following prescribed procedures and requirements' (O'Neill 2002: 49).

Even academics who support audit culture's extension into other professions, after recent self-regulatory breakdowns in the medical, financial, legal and commercial worlds, recoil from the application of such scrutiny to their own world. 'In offices and lecture theatres that are nowadays costed for the purposes of internal budgets, academics confront state-constructed agendas of performance . . . only battery farming of the mind promises that reason will never escape' (Evans 2004: 26–27). Like justice, love and artistry, intellectual activity is viewed as creating value only if pursued for its intrinsic worth. It is devalued if pursued for commercial or career reward, even if these motivations multiply its measured productivity.

These shifts from cloister to knowledge factory, from ivory tower to multiversity, from the privilege of a few to the accumulation of human capital among the many have changed the orientation of most academics. Instead of maintaining an other-worldly front, they now justify their role through the usefulness of knowledge they produce. But universities have not relied on persuasion to ensure that their judgemental dictatorship is viewed as a benign one. Their attainment of centrality to knowledge society, without yielding authority to it, rests on well-developed systems of internal and external control.

Chapter 3

The Extended Educational Enterprise

The channelling of an increasing proportion of school-leavers into higher education, in the belief that this is essential for a modern economy, has changed academia from a reclusive to a socially engaged institution. Ivory towers disappear among science parks and research centres. Academics grow increasingly dependent on consultancy, industrial research grants and cooperation with professions, forcing reflection on real-world problems. Universities have always mixed the pure and the applied, isolated scholars working alongside practising doctors, lawyers and priests. Now they are the central institution in a professionalised world that has redesigned itself around the knowledge they supply.

Increasing engagement can be taken as a sign of success, intellectuals' promotion from observer to driver of economic and social change as their activity rises in value. The majority of academics now compound and apply, train and accredit, rather than originating knowledge. This does not deprive them of prestige. Being involved in the production, validation and application of knowledge, practical as well as theoretical, can gain public respect without losing peer respect, or being drained of its intrinsic rewards.

But having attained the size and influence that go with knowledge monopoly, universities confront two organisational challenges. Internally, they must maintain collegiality and coherence among an increasingly large, diverse spread of subjects and practitioners. Externally, they must guard against distortion and misapplication of knowledge that could discredit its originators. The relaxed internal control required to maintain creativity within the academy can conflict with the tight external control required to maintain authenticity outside it. Organising the creation, validation and dissemination of knowledge to achieve both is a managerial challenge, resolved in a uniquely academic way.

Peer Review vs Public Review

Academics' exercise of control over the status and use of knowledge is not a barrier to their engagement in society. It is the shield that enables such engagement. Church and college have a long-shared expertise at dangling significant truths from the pulpit, without letting the congregation take the law into their own hands. The medieval *secretum secretorium* was a mix of Aristotelian philosophy, occult and alchemy. Priests kept a wary eye on who had access to libraries and which books they could read. Academisation of new subjects stiffened the challenge to traditional control over knowledge, by stretching its applications. The spread of literacy and printing made public science possible. Natural science — coming of age with the foundation of the Royal Society in 1662 and publication of its Philosophical Transactions in 1665 — eventually became a distributed enterprise, interlocking with industrial and government research centres and think tanks. Social science has always been expected to contribute to social wellbeing, and avoid excessive retreat into the academy.

Natural sciences, with their increasingly intricate sub-specialisms, are most prone to peer review's 'small numbers problem'. At very high levels of specialisation and sophistication, only a few researchers worldwide will be properly equipped to judge new work. They will tend to be close colleagues or sworn rivals. With the ability to guess whose latest wisdom they are reviewing comes the ability to backslap friends or backstab enemies — and to steal a sneak preview at the inspirations of both.

Social sciences are prone to the converse problem. Just as televising a football match gives it several million referees, each more adept at spotting infringements than the one on the pitch, disseminating knowledge exposes it to a public audience that is liable to value its own 'review' above that of specialist peers, validating by adoption in everyday use rather than agreement among academic peers. Many natural scientists see their disciplines going the same way if public pressure forces them to separate measles, mumps and rubella vaccines that their research suggests work better together, or to devise additional railway safety measures when evidence tells them the same spent on road safety would save more lives.

The porous boundary of academic social science contrasts with the conventional picture of the sciences, under which reliability is secured by modelling and testing conjectures. The explicit selection, definition and relating of factors, and specification of the boundaries in which the relations hold, enables specialist peers to validate with confidence. From thereon, however, the majority of social scientists are looking for ways of improving the lives of those they study. They prepare and accredit a wide range of professionals and try to inform political and commercial decision-making. The criteria used for judging validity multiply as theoretical insights are compounded and applied.

Peer validation, granted for what is factually or logically supportable, will inevitably deviate from economic validation, based on the capacity for profitable application, or political validation, related to suitability to an administrative agenda. Political or commercial applications of knowledge inevitably mix these knowledge validation criteria. The resultant conflicts quickly surface when academics engage in determining policy or influencing practice. In one long-running example, a task force drawn mainly from academia was established to implement the government's pledge to assess achievement in schools. Sub-committees were established, and research funded. However, the results only partially fulfilled the government's brief, and objections from practitioners soon led to demand for revisions. Costs and timescales increased. When materials were trialled, the teething troubles multiplied. New research was funded, but an innovation would be introduced and revisions made before the academic evaluators reported. Thirty years after national monitoring of achievement in schools became a policy, arbitrary changes were still being demanded and made. The time needed to gather and process data and fulfil a brief means many academic researchers are working on yesterday's problems.

This dismal yet familiar scenario does not reduce the demand for academic research to support decision-making. Academics can still work independently to throw an informed and authoritative light on issues contested by other interested parties. But the complexity of human, including politician, behaviour means that engineering models, problem-centred and tightly controlled, produce misleading results. Acknowledging this, social research increasingly sets out to interpret human behaviour in real rather than experimental situations. Incremental increases in understanding are now expected, not breakthrough solutions and explanations. Validity gains priority over reliability.

Specialists and Special Interests

The need to dig ever deeper for new knowledge, down increasingly narrow shafts, gives a powerful case for entrusting validation to small specialist circles. But the division of intellectual labour invites an uncomfortable parallel with industrial labour division. Industrial productivity leapt when employees were disciplined to do routine tasks, and replaced by machines once the routine became entirely mechanical. Imagination, reflection, discussion, experimentation and non-directed thought, deemed essential to intellectual output, can be deliberately squeezed out by government or industry insisting on the teaching of skills and rigid specifications for research.

Most academics accept a comparison with the broad division of labour, by identifying with a subject category. But they resist a 'Fordist' move to detailed labour division, requiring narrow or repetitious tasks assigned without regard to personal interest and aptitude. Classification as biologist or historian, even as microbiologist or Tudor historian, is acceptable. Within these areas they retain control of the full 'production process', from original research to publication and public presentation. They claim immunity from regulation, even by committees of their own colleagues. The academised intellectual worker thus hopes to avoid the fate of pre-industrial artisans, most of whom lost control of their craft to large-scale manufacturers, and were reduced to turning one small wheel in someone else's vast machine.

Academics expect administration to underwrite their concern with knowledge. They get involved in running the university, and serve on its major committees. They may be subject to formulae for calculating staff numbers, research funds, leave entitlement or supervisory duties, but their priority is to secure the resources to advance specialist interests. From inside, the academy is viewed as an environment of scrutiny and assessment, organised to secure the quality of knowledge production, validation and transmission. Rapid expansion can threaten standards, especially when geared to new applications of specialist knowledge attracting different students. The higher their reputation, the more resistant institutions have generally been to expand research areas or admit new ones. Oxford and Cambridge delayed self-contained recognition of Natural Sciences until late in the nineteenth century, and did not embrace Management Studies until the tail end of the twentieth.

Central to the university environment is a long socialisation of its members through first and higher degrees, postdoctoral research, collaboration in research or professional practice, authorship or co-authorship of papers and attendance at conferences and seminars, acquiring entries on a curriculum vitae and gaining recognition by established figures. This long induction secures membership of the peer group that supports, criticises, validates and ultimately determines career prospects. The structure is hierarchical. In Becher's (1989) study of academics in a dozen specialisms, who they were and where they came from mattered. Institutions, departments, specialisms, individuals were readily ranked, and having an influential patron was an asset. Academics knew whose standing was going up or down, and which stars were worth hitching to. Each specialism had its authority figures, its gatekeepers who control publication, appointment, the allocation of research awards, promotion and honours.

Specialisation enhances the reputation-building that academics claim to be their main incentive, more conducive to useful and unbiased knowledge than financial incentives (Whitley 2000 Ch1–3). It promotes the career security which they claim to be essential for sustained and serious reflection. Differentiation of interests, and of approaches to the same interest, reduces the risk of direct competition. Cases of individuals or teams vying for the same conceptual or empirical breakthrough — as over the structure of DNA and decoding of the human genome — grab headlines precisely because of their rarity value. Researchers more commonly look for subject areas or methods that others are known not yet to have tackled, only duplicating the work of others to check that it has been correctly reported and understood. Indeed, direct competition among scientists is blamed for mistakes, deceptions, wrong turnings and premature publications, more often than it is hailed for speeding knowledge advance. The desire to be first with a major discovery led respected figures to authenticate the Hitler Diaries and Piltdown Man, query the link between HIV and AIDS, suggest one between MMR vaccines and autism, and lay claim to cold nuclear fusion.

Reputation and security are further enhanced by specialisation's insurance against shocks to intellectual consensus. Branches extend incrementally, and rarely make sharp turns. Research is expected to advance knowledge, but in relation to that already validated. Papers are expected to start by reviewing and contextualising themselves in existing literature, and connections are established through copious referencing. Familiarity with the already known is expected by examiners, and subsequent academic careers depend on relating new knowledge to old. There are rewards for innovation, but always within specialist communities, developing a known stock of knowledge in ways that reinforce at least as much as they revise.

Discipline and Publish

Students presenting themselves for examination in thirteenth-century Paris or Bologna defended their theses in an oral tradition that is little changed today. Success meant qualification to teach as a master or doctor. While interrogation has given way to informal talk at some European universities, many stick by the old inquisition. Apparently easygoing relations in a senior common room conceal an academic structure that is not only specialised but hierarchical, differentiated by title and prestige, designed to ensure candidates' cultural as well as intellectual suitability before they get on the tenure track. The performance and publication landmarks that must then be passed, within strict time limits, to stay on course for eventual professorship lift the bar against candidates who take their time or take time out, with especially detrimental effects on the academic representation of women, and anyone forced into earning before higher learning.

Peer assessment determines not only what gets recognised as reliable knowledge, but also who is authorised to generate and teach it. The curriculum vitae, and potted biographies for papers and speaker notes, are finely tuned to win approval from the right intellectual circle. Members know the weight that can be attached to publications, the prestige of committee posts, the status of referees. The unwritten rules by which academics judge other academics retain their priority over any formal criteria that government, industry or professions might try to impose. Those at the base of the pyramid learn to reference their work to peers. Those at the top attract the funds, direct the research and control the output. The common concern with validated knowledge secures both discipline among the many and the authority of a few.

The conventional academic career now often starts at school, where teachers are likely to identify a potential scholar. A first degree externally examined by the eminent Professor Y leads on to a successful Research Council grant application, helped by Y's presence on the relevant Council committee. A PhD is then supervised by a senior lecturer who arranges invitations to attend and read papers at conferences and seminars. Doctoral examination is by Z, a close colleague of Y. The successful student now applies to join specialist research teams, with tutors providing references and discreetly answering informal enquiries. Interview panels can gauge from these associations, as much as the candidate's actual work, whether appointment will generate the required flow of publications, research funds and favourable citations in the chosen specialist area.

The research degree has become the key stage in this academic socialisation. Its purpose has shifted from a genuine venture into uncharted territory, which runs the risk of turning up nothing reportable within the assigned time and budget, to 'research training' that can be judged as successful even in the absence of startling results. Few doctoral theses now become books or launch new subdisciplines. The first lesson in their production is to accumulate references to existing published work. Supervisors ensure that they stay within a specialist canon, and methods are aligned not just to the subject but to prevailing methodological views. Relation to existing work is central to the eventual examination, and failure to reference work deemed central to the subject will be judged a major weakness. Success lies in disciplined departure from existing work, even if the weight of this curtails the length of the forward stride.

At each stage the candidate's main task is to learn the criteria that govern seniors' approval within the chosen specialism. Key tests are formal and infrequent, but informal contacts are continuous. The career starts with a long apprenticeship and can linger on after retirement, with its successive titles of Master, Doctor, Reader, Professor, Dean, Pro Vice-Chancellor and post-retirement Emeritus, all indicators of communal approval for the way the game has been played. Academic socialisation prepares newcomers to think and work as specialists within a hierarchical community, where there is sustained exposure to the scrutiny of others. Adding a new angle to the oft-remarked proximity between genius and madness, Goffman, (1961: 127–69) illustrated this moral pressure through descriptions of patients' experience in mental hospitals. In academia, newcomers seek recognition as 'staff' in identity, self-image and lifestyle. Few other apprenticeships are so long; none is as sustained and intense under the scrutiny of peers.

Public identification with specialised knowledge is distinctive and rewarding, but stressful. Criticism is expected. Rejection is more common than acceptance, especially from top journals. The unpredictability of change and irresistibility of hindsight means few social scientists welcome reference to their published early work. Across a career, especially in social science, many have to reinvent themselves and hope that no-one recalls their initial contributions. Because new disciplines draw their first exponents from other areas of study, or from professions outside academia, their pioneers rarely follow a full career from graduation to retirement. Those that do must stay mentally nimble, or adept at re-interpreting their work, as the world and the way it is theorised keep changing. One advantage of close referencing is that, when thought or action take an unexpected turn, embarrassment is shared with a wider crowd, giving plenty of wrong-footed colleagues to cushion the fall.

Discipline is not the usual characteristic associated with the informal relations, casual dress and flexible timetables of university life. But the rarity of schisms, heresy trials and radical doctrinal disputes in most areas of academia is a tribute to its disciplining power, as much as its ability to settle disputes by definitive test. Sanctions are still available against those who defy normal conventions and noted opinions. Radicalism can potentially lead to enhanced reputation, but also risks withholding of tenure or non-renewal of contract. Discipline, along with extension of specialist interests and peer review of publications, unites the academic profession and excludes the amateur.

The first academic natural and social scientists were often amateurs. Their freedom from specific job titles and departmental affiliations was one factor enabling them to transcend specialism, making polymaths such as Galton and John Stuart Mill impossible to categorise. Some were recruited when they had already delivered major results or laid the groundwork for a research programme. As the twentieth century progressed, amateur contributions became ever rarer, their authors shut out of shared conversation, mutual referencing and peer recognition. Today a CV with the right referees, journal appearances and institutional affiliations is essential for admission to jobs, referee networks and selection panels, confirming recognised status within a specialist academic community and showing that the necessary discipline has been learned.

Karl Marx (1818–83) fled various university departments under political and philosophical fire, and ended up working in the library of the British Museum, with occasional field trips to Friedrich Engels' factories. Marx would have found it difficult to be as productive or subversive in a contemporary university, which would certainly have queried his frequent diversion into pamphlets that can't be counted towards the research assessment exercise, and predilection for taking time off to organise Communist Internationals with no clear conference theme. But once published, Marx's work — the polemical as well as the more scholarly — became a major influence on economics, sociology, history and philosophy.

Nathan Isaacs (1895–1966) exposed the extent to which, in less than a century, ideas' origin and form of presentation had become as important as their content in establishing their validity. As a metals importer helping his first wife, Susan, run the influential Malting House School in Cambridge, Isaacs attempted to publish on the relation between philosophy and psychology. His books and articles submitted between 1920 and 1960 were continually rejected by academic editors and referees, mainly citing his failure to reference ongoing academic work, use conventional definitions or condense to normal length. Isaacs' fortunes changed only when he contributed to his first wife's books in the early 1930s, and moved closer to conventional format. After this he was able to publish numerous academic journal articles and exert a major influence on English primary education through his evidence to the Plowden Committee, translations of Piaget and involvement (via his second wife) in the National Froebel Foundation. However, his influence was brief, as teacher education then became academised. In the last quarter of the twentieth century, dreamers and doers were replaced by knowers, disciplined by peer evaluation within the expanding archive of academically approved work.

Exclusion or absorption of the amateur moved the academy closer to monopolisation of knowledge. Universities provided laboratories, administrative support, cost-effective aggregations of students and other practical, productivity-related reasons for amateurs to move inside them. But they also offered more pragmatic incentives: access to archives, inside knowledge of unpublished work, the criticism and support of specialist peers. These controlled access to prestigious, refereed publications and hence to academic audiences. Amateurs who rejected this discipline had to keep addressing a popular audience, and so were on the wrong side of the border when academics started to draw one between their own and ordinary views of the world.

Managing the Multiversity

Successful companies come under relentless pressure to expand: re-investing profits from existing activities to develop or acquire new ones, expanding market and customer share. The fastest of these virtuous circles can transform a garage start-up into a global brand-name within the founders' lifetime. But growth carries risks — of expanding operations faster than the resources needed to manage them, making wrong technological turnings, or taking on activities outside the area of expertise. Sometimes the over-reaching hand swiftly regains magic touch. Equally often, the lithe specialist becomes an atrophied conglomerate, or the jack of all trades gets defeated by an ace in each one.

Successful countries can encounter similar 'imperial overstretch' as economic growth widens their political sphere of influence, creating scope and incentive to dominate other nations. Extraterritorial strength is initially self-reinforcing, turning national power into 'superpower' with influence and interests disproportionate to size. But superpowers are then sidetracked into adventures abroad that cost more in security bills than they deliver in wealth or prestige, once the subordinated nations and cultures start wrestling with the one that grew too much.

Universities have mirrored these expansionary hazards, despite their occupants' general dislike of commercial or political empire building. Their solution to the decision-making delays and coordination failures that often undermine rapid growth has been essentially the same as that of large companies: the switch from unitary to multiply centred organisation. Each activity is given operational and budgetary autonomy within a loosely federated structure, with central management setting overall strategy and resource allocation. Clark Kerr, heading the University of California as it grew into the world's largest study and research complex, recognised and rejoiced in *The Uses of the Multiversity* (1963). 'Multiversalisation' seemed the way ahead for organised knowledge creation, once the community of scholars no longer clustered in one place, or spoke a common language. While much maligned, especially after Kerr called the police to defend his organisation against rebel students later in the 1960s, his vision has been implicitly accepted by all large universities. Most now occupy multiple sites, especially after mergers with other tertiary institutions. Many disciplines celebrate their coming of age by escaping the incubating faculty, moving to new buildings where older voices can no longer interrupt.

The academic enterprise gives physical expression to the claim that production and validation of knowledge is the business of academics, not to be dictated by bishops, governments, funding agencies, industrial sponsors or fee-paying students. Collegiate authority is maintained over course content, quality of research, teaching and assessment method, even in the most vocationally orientated multiversity. This claim to autonomy had to be re-defined as the small and still essentially medieval colleges of the nineteenth century expanded and departmentalised in the twentieth, shaking off their religious influences. Academics moved from being an elite in a largely uneducated society to a key professional group, preparing and accrediting others for managing, educating, caring and curing. In a specialised world, academics cover the whole gamut of knowledge, providing a common cultural background and doing much of the fundamental thinking for society at large.

Beneath this unifying feature the contemporary multiversity is highly specialised, with faculties' differentiation and fragmentation (into Arts, Humanities, Education, Natural and Social Science) transmitting upwards to their central organisation. Faculties invoke powers of the mind. But their increasing subdivision into institutes, centres, schools, departments and committees undermines any claim that knowledge's parts add up to a unified whole. The arrival of new disciplines further impedes coherence and logical classification. Social Psychology can be found in faculties of Science, Biological and Agricultural Sciences, Humanities, Education or Health and Medicine. Economists are often displaced into the Business School or Management Centre, sociologists into Cultural or Human Studies.

The variety in university prospectuses illustrates this scope. At the start of the twenty-first century about three-quarters of the hundred plus British universities offered degree courses in economics and in psychology and two-thirds in sociology. All have acquired their distinctive content, as courses 'modularise' in parallel with (and under pressure from) the specialisation of research. One sociology department may offer family relations and the church in medieval France, or women's history and gender relations in the Soviet Union. Next door, economics students can opt for the influence of German Romanticism on economic behaviour, or the contemporary relevance of Malthus. Staff members' particular specialisms and interests usually provide the basis for such differentiation. While students may be seeking a generic degree, universities welcome any chance to distinguish themselves on course content, so as to avoid head-to-head competition over quality or price.

Fragmentation and Modularisation

The majority of students now entering academia will follow combined, modular, interdisciplinary, or professional courses such as business, media, women's, cultural or leisure studies. These draw on many specialisms within different social sciences, linking the strands from different disciplines that relate to work and sport, government and community, childhood and old age, culture and media, sickness and health, investment and poverty. One typical university prospectus now claims to offer over fifty subjects and 'thousands of ways in which they can be combined to allow you to customise your programme of study'. Eight or nine modules are taken in each year, as major, minor, joint or independent, with a choice of pathways through them, and 24 are needed to graduate. If they can navigate the maze and complete a good first degree, the 200,000 students entering postgraduate courses each year can go deeper into Corporate and International Finance, Family Therapy, Social Gerontology, Life Course Development or Gender and Modernism. Large numbers who had never intended to study social science will be forcibly acquainted with selected insights during professional courses for business, management, social work, teaching, counselling or childcare.

University bureaucracies prevent this curricular and organisational mosaic degenerating into an entirely abstract art. They pigeonhole the specialised knowledge, fashioning it into components of more systematic study programmes. Each component is of known quality, secured through the long process of academic induction and qualification. The preservation of depth despite ever increasing breadth is not easy. Results are more often analogous to a patchwork than the fish-scales and honeycombs evoked in prospectuses, as students are left to decipher the connection between the options. Their ability to do so becomes one of the tests on the way to their qualification.

Curricular diversity helps to attract new resources and develop new areas for research. It reduces the tension between academic interests, and diffuses the pressure from external auditing. The need to attract money for research and development means a rising tide of demands and recommendations from specialisms to departments to faculty boards and up into the central administration. Here academics replay any competing demands not reconciled at a lower level. Detached from internal battles between knowledge branches, universities' central committees are more alive to the external constraints imposed by government, industry, professions and the marketplace, failure to deal with which would be a threat to academic freedom. University councils, usually with a majority of lay members, traditionally rarely challenged academic decisions despite their formal control over the senate. They have been forced to take a tougher line as external constraints make internal conflicts more frequent and damaging. Vice-chancellors and principals are increasingly selected for commercial and political experience as much as for academic pedigree.

As well as keeping order within their activities, multiversities try to influence the markets for their services. Public relations are managed through increasingly glossy prospectuses and interactive websites; advertising and recruiting are organised internationally. Academics are expected to join the sales force, exploiting publicity opportunities even if not aspiring to the status of media don. Those who once asserted their own intellectual property rights must now share them with their institution, for which commercial exploitation of patent and copyright is an increasingly valuable source of reputation and income. But in relation to knowledge itself, academics strive to retain independence. Overt managerial authority coordinating production, validation and application is resented and resisted. Specialists defend their boundaries, battling non-specialist or administrative interference, often referring it to ethics committees. Even in the modern buildings of new universities, ancient universities' feudal and monastic traditions recur.

This mix of the feudal and modern accounts for the attractions and tensions of the academic life. Authority and threats to it come from the same source. Specialist insight is adapted as it is compounded for application. Peers judge the validity of knowledge, but cannot determine its application. Validation is by specialist peers using their own criteria and references, but these alter along the way from the production to the retailing of knowledge. It is then applied beyond academia in ways that often distress those who first produced it.

Conclusion: The Invincible Hand

Academia's strength is in validating knowledge through a traditional culture. Its increasingly visible weakness arises from unresolved dependence on demand, from students for courses that promise well-regarded employment, and for research output with profit-making potential. The resulting tension is expressed in the contemporary labels of knowledge factory, McDonaldisation (Ritzer, 2000), multiversity, periversity, and post-academic now attached. The concern is that knowledge itself is distorted or destroyed in the process of managerialisation and marketisation. The incursion of market pressures takes physical form in the concentration of hi-tech firms on and around campus. Universities are encouraged by government to cooperate with industry, competing for funds from private and public sectors, with ownership of knowledge increasingly disputed as those who underwrote it look for a return on their investment.

Institutionalised human ingenuity is no guarantee of enlightenment. To Habermas (1972), the rationality manifested in the eighteenth century bourgeois salon is now perverted by the development of capitalist media that deal in knowledge as a commodity and package it for popular consumption. Many view Kerr's 'multiversity' as a similarly malign bureaucratisation, recalling a golden age before colleges lost autonomy and lecturers succumbed to publication targets. But to condemn the trend as 'refeudalisation', because an expanded forum must work through channels that might distort the message, is to exaggerate the virtues of the forum before its growth required such channelling. The salon was the preserve of a tiny minority. Today a majority acquire and use theoretical knowledge, with 'reflective practitioners' often advancing the subject faster than non-practising reflectors.

Evidence and ideas once confined to top tables have now become a part of everyday life, bringing potential for the enlightened, critical use of knowledge to a majority. While accused of reshaping public opinion, feudal media barons often struggle to reflect it. Journalists complain of their mediating power being challenged as new communication channels make everyone a source of news and comment, letting low-cost digests and interpretations expand at the expense of costly original production of information. The rising volume of commercially driven secondary analysis and application places a premium on the value of original knowledge, and on primary research shielded from economic and political pressure. Status as societies' pathfinder through the information explosion enhances the academy's investigative and interpretive power. Through disciplined internal activity and a carefully managed external impact, apparently democratised higher education has gained unprecedented influence on the way people, and those who govern or employ them, think and act.

Chapter 4

Models, Metaphors and Mediation

The most popular spectator sports are those at which, a century ago, gifted amateurs could have tackled the professionals and not been totally embarrassed. Today the fans can still shout tactical advice from the sidelines, but know they would be crushed if they stepped beyond them. Modern professionals, with their years of training and tactical discipline, are in a different league. The academic spectacle has undergone a similar transformation, on a matching timescale. Until the World Wars, better students could already be contributing to cutting-edge debate before completing undergraduate study. Interested readers could scan a refereed journal without being floored by the algebraic or linguistic abstractions. Today's intellectuals have taken the game to a level comprehensible only to specialists. Theirs is a different world, with unfamiliar glossaries, taxonomies and conventions, even if its physical location has shifted from campus into community. They have moved beyond the reach of the mass while simultaneously educating increasing numbers, directly through their teaching and indirectly through informing public debate.

Today we live in a world increasingly less perceived in terms of heaven and hell, and more rationalised through secular models, often originating in academia. Daughters-in-law view their partners differently once aware of the Oedipus complex. Drivers change their cornering after learning of centres of gravity and centrifugal force. Pay negotiators alter their tone once taught to visualise supply and demand curves for labour, with their market-clearing wage rate. Candlelit trysts take a new turn when he and she find themselves at opposite ends of the psychometric spectrum. Representations of the world, crafted as an aid to intellectual thought, have profound effects when fused into popular consciousness. The impact is heightened, and made more dangerous, by the widening gap between models as professionally developed and as popularly applied.

Models and Reality

Simplified and stylised accounts of reality, which exaggerate the features under study and omit or minimise those judged irrelevant, appeared early in the natural sciences. Their success at moving subjects on, from the retrieved world of Aristotle to the revealed world of Copernicus and Newton, ensured their rapid import into the nascent social sciences. Ricardo's model showing the all-round virtues of international trade still appears in textbooks, more than a century after its formulation. Models of the mind and the body politic have had shorter shelf-lives, but their impact has been central, and leaves its permanent mark even when the diagrams and mechanisms change.

Models mediate between reality and theory, between our perceptions of what happens in the world and the thoughts and expectations we generate about it. Their lack of realism is often presented as a strength — like that of maps, whose clarity grows the more they put simple symbols in place of complex terrain. So many objects and events exist around us, connected in so many possible ways, that merely contemplating the world is a recipe for confusion. Observation depends on preconceived ideas of what to look for and expect. The preconceptions with which we approach the world are more model-laden than theory-laden. Interpretive templates with which people recognise and respond to their situations can be derived inductively from theory, or deductively from observation and triggered recollection.

Models also mediate between theory and reality, helping to relate our thoughts and expectations back to the world. Theorisation about the world, natural or social, or the individual, tends to get more complex over time. If not in content, then in linguistic or mathematical form, formal expressions of theory start to surpass the understanding of non-specialist observers. A model can add coherence to theories by bringing them together, to shed light on the problem in focus from more than one angle. It can also weave a story around theories, giving them a sense not grasped from their formal expression, and bringing them to life.

When first deployed, models were intended to help perceive the real world more clearly: the landscape through the fog, or the wood for the trees. While abstracted from reality, models aimed at better representing it, not replacing it. Early models in physics and chemistry worked largely as simplified representations — an object as a point mass, bouncing balls as atoms of gas. But natural scientists' models, especially when translated to mathematics, quickly ceased to be directly representative. Those of social scientists, being about abstract entities rather than tangible realities, were generally unrepresentative from the start. With realistic representation removed from models' desiderata, their relevance came to be judged mainly by accurate prediction of future results, or 'retrodiction' of already observed results. With this transition, models ceased to hold up just a mirror or a magnifying lens. From seeing the world *through* models, researchers began to see the world *in* models. Arguments came to be stated and tested in terms of the framework, not of the world that this had been designed to represent.

In step with this change, model building that once lurked as a hidden assumption became fully explicit, and what had been a complement to academic study was made a necessary component. Many papers that would once have embedded the model in a wider, mainly verbal discussion now launch straight into its specification. All the main results and conclusions are derived and assessed within the model. Often only a short introductory and valedictory paragraph link it to the wider world, and relate the conclusions back to that world.

From Representation to Reification

The exploitation of models facilitates understanding of complexity. Building a hydraulic model of the economy on Keynesian lines can simplify the relation between input and output, saving and investment. Organic models of human society can yield fascinating ideas about social roles and functional relations. Modelling the mind as a computer can suggest ways in which humans process information. Each model may only be transitory, as humans interpret and scientists respond. But the concepts and their relations reinforce the influence of academics, since only they can fully understand, and rearrange, the particular lenses through which the laity now perceive the world.

In each case there is a tendency to slip from model to reality. Models are simplified, synthetic, often precise and free of contexts. They are useful but never match the complexity of the social. They have to be changed as their impact is felt. Yet their influence has been sufficient for them to be accepted not just as guides to understanding but as real features, 'out there', waiting to be observed. Market forces, intelligence, social class are treated as if they existed independent of the way they have been constructed. Their loss of precision, in the series of transfers from academic producer to retailer and on to users, can promote their conformity to experience that accepts them as real.

Whenever metaphors or models are used convincingly, they are open to reification. Academics gain public recognition by applying their theories to everyday events. Professionals use these ideas to maintain influence in relation to clients. They become the currency of newscasters, playwrights and authors. In everyday life we work things out by thinking 'as if'. Academic modelling is differentiated only by its precision and assessment by experts. Even then, most academic models are soon amended or rejected. The labour theory of value, 'g' factor intelligence and historical materialism brought prestige to those who devised and first applied them. They rapidly entered professional and political practice, becoming part of the way everyday events were explained. Their reification meant they persisted in everyday use long after academics had heavily revised or rejected them.

The confusion of model with reality can become a major problem in professional and lay thought and action, especially in relation to the social world. First, it can enable ideas to survive — often unacknowledged — in popular discourse long after they are abandoned by the originators. Social scientists are involved in the world they study. They can change models overnight. Simultaneously, thinking humans are also constructing and changing their working models, increasingly using social scientific ideas. The appetite for models, and keenness to accept and apply them, reflects our thirst to know about ourselves. Reification is reassuring to the users, who can assume they are discussing reality, and flattering to the academics, for whom this enhances authority.

The reification of 'intelligence' after construction of the first tests by Binet and their development by Terman at the start of the twentieth century, made them important instruments in educational policy and practice. The Intelligence Quotient (IQ) took on a facticity as concrete as the Chronological Age; multiplying the two and dividing by 100 produced the Mental Age. On this basis, children with an IQ below 85 were classified as 'dull and backward', below 70 as 'educationally subnormal' and below 50 as ineducable, while those above 120 deserved a grammar-school education. Use of such scores extended into employment decisions, immigration control and even decisions on whether those with learning difficulties should procreate. Belief in IQ became so entrenched that leading psychologist Cyril Burt falsified evidence to defend the tests' validity. Decades after the underlying concept of intelligence fixed at birth was rejected by the British Psychological Society and in academia, it is still widespread in everyday discourse, and in the memory of teachers and social workers. It had appeared to offer a 'scientific' way to select for an increasingly differentiated school system. Professionals facing an urgent problem can build an ambitious programme on a shaky platform, to justify actions that later seem abusive or absurd.

Second, reification uses the authority of academia to reinforce the confidence that we can know. The global market, intelligence, social class, subconscious motives enter discussion as if they were real, not just intellectual constructs. Applications of thought that should supply tests of the model that inspired it become adaptations of thought that help confirm the model. Academics act as artists as much as scientists, imaginatively building models that have elegance as well as explanatory power. They can give the world meaning and make its exploration exciting. But they are still models — a distinction especially likely to be lost when human agency enters the model. Decision theorists, faced with numerous cases in which even well-educated subjects with full information fail to make the 'rational' choice, tend to stand by their model and suggest better training to help people conform to it.

Third, changes inside, across and outside academia do not necessarily move in step. It takes time for academic knowledge to be compounded and applied. Managers, social workers and teachers can be influenced by models already buried in the academic archives. Ideas can be changed even before their reified versions have been built into professional training and practice, and common sense. Academic models relating social interaction and learning influenced investment in school buildings and equipment, and the training of teachers, that took decades to replace. High-rise apartment blocks, originally promoted for their social benefits, likewise linger on city skylines decades after sociological consensus has shifted to low-rise estates, or rehabilitated the back-to-back 'slum'.

Fourth, ordinary people also model and change their world, sometimes rejecting or reconfiguring an academic model in ways that catch its originators by surprise. Black activists and feminists exposed stereotypes and attitudes in advance of academics in the 1960s. Textbook representations of the typical agent as a white, Anglo-Saxon Protestant 'he' are now an indelible reminder of the unacknowledged preconceptions. British social reformers a century ago sought to bring new social and material rights to the empire and the servant classes, not seeing that the full extension of their values required the end of empire and elimination of the master-servant divide. Academics can be slow to acknowledge the established canon as a barrier to change. Yet at any one time there will be ascending and descending models both in academia and in everyday discourse. Academics are most secure when probing the redundancy of their predecessors' models. Users of models have more of an interest in their durability. Thinkers' joy in continual turnover of ideas clashes with practitioners' desire for stable expectations and practices.

Models and Internalised Conversation

Agreement on a model creates a common language for research. Specialists in a particular field who converge on the same model can now agree on their view of the world, and acknowledge its background assumptions so that these need no longer clutter the discussion. The model provides a private language in which experts can communicate more quickly and precisely, assimilating new ideas and transmitting results faster than if they stayed with the language and concepts of the 'real world'. A shared model lets specialists move straight to substantive discussion: on how associations between variables can be calibrated and rationalised as cause and effect; on what aspects of the model need further testing, what data this will require, and what restrictive assumptions could be usefully changed or relaxed. For example, a long debate between Monetarist and Keynesian economics was eventually boiled down to conflicting beliefs about one variable, the sensitivity of money demand to changes in interest rates. Models help to pinpoint the main disagreements between approaches to a subject. This opens the way, in the natural sciences, to a defining experiment that will establish which is right, or in the social sciences to crystallisation of opinion around a 'mainstream' approach.

Academic models are ideally parsimonious and precise. The units, factors and variables need not be reflections of the real world. Modern physics and economics, in particular, claim explanatory success in inverse proportion to the realism of their models. The more closely and narrowly a model is defined, the greater the agreement among users on what they are investigating and validating. Precision reduces complexity, leads to testable hypotheses, facilitates peer evaluation and points the way to further work. With a shared focus for assessment, specialists can judge one another's work according to the internal development of the model as much as the realism of its assumptions or applicability of its predictions.

The spread of model-based thinking is promoted by the steep hierarchy of scholarly communities, in which a broad, untenured base of doctoral and postdoctoral researchers ascends to a rarefied peak of multiple professorship holders and Nobel laureates. The stars distinguish themselves through publication, conference appearances and rapid promotion. Those on lower rungs tolerate the large status differences because they hope to benefit from exposure to the brighter minds, eventually rising to similar heights — and because well-grasped hands in high places can help haul them to the top. Collegiality reflecting shared interest is reinforced by shared distinction from the world around. Common assumptions, definitions and models help graded minds think alike. The consequent tribal or village atmosphere can become oppressive and factionalised, but is defended as best balancing the cooperation and competition needed for knowledge to advance. Advances in communication strengthen the safeguards against insularity by globalising such networks.

The idea of a constraining and enabling 'paradigm' as the focus of normal science has been hard to escape since Kuhn (1962) proclaimed *The Structure of Scientific Revolutions*. Shared values, assumptions, models and procedures that define scholarly communities' membership and conduct are recognised even by those strongly critical of the paradigm's conceptual malleability and historical accuracy. Thus Lakatos (1978), while keen to defend Karl Popper's more decontextualised and rigorous view of scientific method, describes the 'research programme' determining the agenda for a scholarly community. Such communities have been described as transepistemic areas of research (Knorr-Cetina, 1982), as networks, research traditions (Laudan, 1977), and as models of linked concepts defended by groups because of their promise (Hesse, 1980). All suggest the same specialised, close-knit, self-validating, mutually-referencing group as the basic unit of academia. The medieval scholar would recognise both the satisfaction and the tension involved.

Worlds Apart

The obverse side of easier conversation between subscribers to a shared model is increased gulfs of understanding between groups adhering to different models. Communication requires a group to translate the others' ideas into the terms of its own model. The other groups almost invariably complain that such translation loses crucial aspects of their argument — and offer a translation of other models into their terms that is equally objectionable to rival camps. Before the redefinition of disciplines around shared models, academia resembled a lingua franca planet. Everyone could make their basic meanings understood; but their imperfect knowledge of — and spatial and temporal variations in — the universal language and its accompanying gestures made for frequent misunderstanding, and an inability to convey detailed meanings with certainty or precision.

Once models become embedded, academia changes to a world in which each like-minded group speaks its own distinct language. Their comprehension of, and ability to work with, others in the group is substantially enhanced. Their ability to talk meaningfully to other groups, and share ideas with them, is equally substantially reduced. All depend on assumptions, analogies, metaphors and models as ways of reducing the complexity in order to theorise. In academia these models, explicit and precise or implicit and loose, serve as a focus for a community of scholars. They also serve as a gateway to further specialisation, for even minor changes to assumptions can result in big changes to theories and redundancy in applications.

The progressive concentration of academics around shared models, mutually assessing the quality of their specialised knowledge production, can be seen in the history of the London School of Economics from its establishment at the start of the twentieth century. Initially there were no departmental labels, and first appointees taught across subject boundaries that would now be viewed as unbridgeable. Dahrendorf (1995a; 1995b) describes windows on the same sight, giving different perspectives but a 'unity of intent'. Social science at LSE began to dissolve from the 1920s, as Economics, Political Science, Social Anthropology, Social Psychology and Sociology became separate departments. In the second half of the century each subject developed subdisciplines, and degree courses split further into options. Specialisation was seen to be dividing social science and divorcing it from the humanities. The fragmentation of theory accompanied increasingly diverse applications to business, management, caring and counselling, education, organisation and community.

Models are justified by the need to isolate, from a complex reality, those elements directly relevant to the puzzle being probed. They specify the links between those elements, eliminating irrelevant items or connections, enabling focus on the direction of causation and the scale of its effects. But from being a means to understanding and depicting the world beyond, models can easily become ends in themselves, capturing researchers' attention to the exclusion of that world. Choice of model can also signify a wider intellectual choice, over which discipline to enter, which method to apply, which received wisdom to subscribe to, which institutions to join and which individuals to select as peers. A shared model is often at the heart of the 'paradigms' that shape the scientists' choice of what to study and how to interpret it, and determine who else can understand and judge their work. Academic discussion becomes conducted in models that are not routinely related back to reality, or cannot be related without sparking further discussion which jumps back into the framework of the decontextualised model.

Thus models affect what researchers look for and expect to observe, and the interpretation they place on what is observed. Research conducted through the preconceptions of a model will tend to reinforce its assumptions. Unorthodox economists have long complained that the available data, on such variables as production, prices, costs, profits, industrial and occupational classifications, reflects categorisations informed by mainstream models and so cannot provide neutral tests of these or alternative models. The expense of data collection means that it must generally be publicly funded, allowing the mainstream to strengthen its ascendancy by confining data sets to those most supportive of its models. The same problem befalls scientists who wish to test highly unorthodox theories, such as the ascent of prices without monetary expansion or the descent of humans from aquatic apes. Thought constraints imposed by a model, like the behavioural constraints imposed by an organisation, promote 'single-loop learning' (Argyris & Schon 1978), under which novel information or observation is assimilated within the framework of present assumptions, objectives and rules. Considerable effort is needed to move to the 'double-loop learning' under which anomalous results lead to a revision of these underlying model parameters.

Entry into the 'double loop' often requires the recognition and re-articulation of norms and values that have become ingrained and unspoken, so that those governed by them no longer recognise their influence. A gap can open up between the theory people say they are applying and the theory they actually apply, which may not be noticed until unexpected experiences force deeper reflection. Because it shapes the evidence used for testing, the language used for discussion and the unstated assumptions behind that discussion, modelling reality means modifying reality. Conversation among those with shared belief in a particular model becomes unintelligible to those who lack such belief, to whom the others appear to be living in a different world.

Epistemic and Interpretive Shifts

Models can filter out irrelevant aspects of the subject under study and magnify the relevant aspects, presenting a clearer view than is available through unmediated observation. But the filter can exclude aspects that other theories consider relevant. The lens can blow other features up out of proportion. Viewing the world through its currently fashionable models can quickly become like trying to tour London using only its famous Underground map.

In principle, a model can be tested against reality, and so rejected if it consistently fails to describe or predict that reality. The geocentric model of the universe proved untenable when confronted with ever more detailed observation of planetary movements, despite ingenious modifications to try to account for these. The Keynesian model of aggregate demand, output and prices in an economy, although given physical form by postwar followers as a hydraulic circulation that initially held water, was abandoned when additional demand was seen to be fuelling inflation rather than raising real output — or when the pipes sprang a leak. But most models, including these, withstand many contradictions before being called into question, and an increasing number can avoid such testing altogether.

Natural-science models achieve this insulation through an 'epistemic shift', in which the way we know (the model) distracts attention from what we know (the modelled). The world against which a model is tested may not be the 'real' world, but merely a representation of it. That representation may not accurately depict the reality. It may even be shaped by the model it is meant to test. 'Realists' charge that models tested against surface observation may falsely identify regularities, and infer causal links, ignoring deeper structures that may underlie the observable world of objects and events, and are not directly observable. To realist critics, model-building enables (and disguises) a shift from ontological reasoning about the nature of the world, and our existence in it, to epistemological reasoning about our knowledge of that world, and of the way we exist.

Social-science models reinforce the insulation with an 'interpretive shift', in which the assumptions and information held by the modeller are pushed into the head of those modelled. Model-consistent expectations — those relating to aggregate outcomes which agents need to hold in order to generate those aggregate outcomes — underpin orthodox economic theory(ies), which gives them the alias of 'rational expectations' to emphasise the absurdity of thinking otherwise. The assumption is that anyone who acts on expectations that the model fails to fulfil will quickly adapt, until they and other agents alight on expectations that generate actions which lead to their fulfilment.

The experience of economists' search for 'general equilibrium' reveals the limits of this superficially attractive proposition. Many people are reluctant to abandon initial expectations and slow to adapt. If those who initially get closer to the expectation that would be model-consistent (if everyone shared it) are also faster to adapt, they may move away from that expectation faster than those acting inconsistently with it move towards it. Even where they can prove the existence of a situation in which everyone acts on expectations that get fulfilled, economists must make some heroic assumptions before the price mechanism, their traditional mechanism for learning and adaptation, leads people there. A model that presupposes full information, unlimited power to process it, markets for everything and no economies of large scale strikes many as assuming most of the things they would like economics to explain.

Assumptions, models and metaphors are universal ways to understand the complex by use of the simple. The academy absorbed rather than originated model-based enquiry. While few social scientists enjoy comparison of their craft with literary criticism, Shakespeare can be credited with having invented the human (Bloom 1999), by making dramatic relations reflexive. The world's a stage, its men and women merely players. Social science shares this reflexive view of the human, making central use of metaphor. It is easy to slip from constructing reality metaphorically to treating it as actually out there, independent of any modelling. Markets, supply and demand, intelligence, emotion, motivation, race, class and gender are constructs, though all can be accepted as factual. The modelling of humans as social beings constructing their own reality has its hero in Erving Goffman (1961). In mental hospitals, military establishments, prisons, isolated communities and schools, humans find ways of interacting to make life tolerable. While it may have lost favour in psychology and sociology, this 'ethogenic' approach (Harré, 1993) reappears in more fashionable disciplines — the consumer identity warred over by marketing science, the impression management taught in business schools.

Communication, Reduction and Commodification

Models promote a deductive approach to knowledge creation, setting out assumptions from which the subject studied can be examined and its workings explained. That is a metaphorical and universal human way to understanding, employed by philosopher, poet, scientist and everyday gossip. Humans have produced a plentiful supply in their urge to know, some disciplined to form the basis of academic modelling. Here the titles gestalt, macro, holistic, structural, systemic, functional indicate a broad, embracing, top-down focus. Such 'macro' models that depict a whole system are generally an assembly of, or aggregation across, sub-models that focus on its parts. But models can also be used reductively, tracing the complexity of the observed world to underlying regularities, and identifying the subset of relevant variables whose interaction generates the aggregate effects.

Most academic models' explanatory and persuasive power lies in the isolation of a component of a system, treating others as absent or holding them constant. This reduction also hastens the 'horizontal' fragmentation of knowledge into disciplines, by providing rules for membership of different communities with different archives and assumptions. This also encourages the 'vertical' fragmentation of knowledge, by dividing each discipline into levels of analysis of which the lowest, most elementally divided is usually regarded as the most fundamental.

Reductionism invites the powerful objection of failing to allow for 'emergent' phenomena, in systems whose aggregate or subsequent results are unpredictable from their base-level or initial conditions. But the general response to any 'fallacy of composition' — mistaken prediction of the whole from behaviour patterns of the parts — has often been to improve the model's bottom-up mechanics, not replace it with a top-down alternative. Reductionist approaches speed up knowledge production by promoting academic specialisation, and by encouraging the search for 'microfoundations' within each specialism. Chemistry was reformulated and revolutionised with the atom as its basic building-block, biology with the gene, economics with the rational maximising agent, international relations with the nation-state, linguistics with the phoneme. However, while these undisputable successes have ensured its spread to other disciplines, reductionism breeds a Trojan horse when applied to the knowledge creation process itself, particularly when used in studying the human.

By 'atomising' knowledge, reductionism promotes its commodification. Separated from their originators and divided into small units, ideas are opened to the same economic possibilities as industrial products: to be stored, accumulated, traded, recombined, used as collateral, or turned into capital from which further ideas can flow. For example, modelling of transmissible mental products has recently been revived through the concept of 'memes', whose impact on mental and cultural evolution is compared to that of biological evolution's genes. Academics have not been slow to see how deeply this model of cultural transmission can undermine established social scientific models. But social scientific ideas are never buried for long. The human condition is so complex and fascinating that there are hundreds of models extant, many more to be dug out of archives or constructed.

'Memetic' transmission is an alternative to the 'didactic' approach, in which ideas must be acquired from their original source. The didactic has made steady inroads into the memetic, as academy-centred tuition has replaced learning on the job or in informal interaction (Dawkins, 1989: 192). Yet word can travel much faster if students can pass it to other students, rather than having to hear it from the professor. The higher speed and lower cost of memetic transmission explains its growing popularity in marketing, where propagating 'word of mouth' can be more cost-effective than placing advertisements. Away from advertising, however, information is easier to trust if received from distant experts rather than close friends. Academisation is encouraged in part by the belief that skills and reasoning learnt in college carry an authority not possessed by the colleague who shows you on the job. The accreditation attained by formal instruction is needed to find employment with these skills, if not actually to acquire them.

Memetic transmission of ideas, like the genetic transmission of traits, has notable shortcomings compared with the didactic alternative. First, popularity is no guarantee of quality. Second, memes are likely to misrepresent or misinterpret ideas. Constant reference back to source may slow the spread of the idea, but enables academics to avoid the spread of ideas beyond the time and place of their original inspiration. Third, memetic transmission takes place beyond the reach of those who first sowed the ideas, so nobody can be credited or held responsible for the authenticity of the original knowledge creation. Fourth, while memetics requires information in small, portable packets, didactics works equally well with knowledge that cannot be codified or broken down into component parts. Fifth, memetic transmission may be effective only for more basic, less 'sophisticated' ideas, becoming the stuff of catchy tunes that distract us from serious compositions. Sixth, memetic knowledge can spread where culturally contextualised didactic knowledge is context-bound. Academia has thrived on the belief that while memes may be an inevitable vehicle for pop tunes and gossip, reliable knowledge transmission still calls for a didactic approach.

Underlying all the above objections is the conviction that while memetic knowledge transmission is easier, quicker and cheaper than didactic transmission, it is of inferior quality. A situation where life's more trivial secrets transmit memetically, leaving bigger ideas to be spelt out didactically, could even work to academia's advantage. But whispers at the back of the lecture hall have always distressed those on the rostrum. Having based so much of their growth on the replacement of word-of-mouth with word-of-prof, academics treasure their knowledge-disseminating exclusivity. But it can be achieved at high cost, tipping pursuit of excellence into arrogance. Sartre's contempt for the Autodidact who contributes to his *Nausea*, the obscurity of Thomas Hardy's *Jude*, and the mercilessness of E.M. Forster (a Cambridge 'Apostle') against the literary pretensions of Leonard Bast in *Howard's End* typify the worse-than-uselessness intellectuals ascribe to any self-improvement efforts not sponsored and selected by themselves.

Conclusion: Surpassing All Understanding

The emergence of an interpretive elite, and their pursuit of knowledge down ever narrower disciplines into ever finer detail, has widened the gulf between academic reasoning and public understanding just as popular higher education is being organised. The top natural science journals were already, a century ago, ceasing to be intelligible even to the best educated lay audience. Top social science journals have made the same transition out of ordinary language within the past half century, mostly through the deployment of ever more complex terminology, maths and statistics. Top humanities journals are now achieving the same translation, sometimes into comparable symbolic logic, more often into modified language in which words and phrases transcend their everyday meaning and normal grammatical rules do not apply. Much academic writing (and equationing) is now incomprehensible even to other academics in apparently related fields.

Incomprehensibility to wider audiences does not however necessarily mean irrelevance to them. Because specialisation drives knowledge creation, it can even be an index of value. To be dazzled by science is an acceptable side-effect of labour division in knowledge production, if the main effect is to be comforted, enriched, excited or cured by science. People can see the usefulness of, and get pleasure from, an intellectual product — be it a games console or a game-theory concept — with only a cursory understanding of how it works. Indeed, the more rarefied is the knowledge a gadget contains, the less we tend to worry about not knowing what goes on inside it.

But applied knowledge's ability to gain in sophistication without losing the common touch relies on there being clarity on what the product does, and why it is valuable. Pure knowledge producers risk losing public trust once they surpass public understanding, if the purpose of their discoveries becomes as obscure as the way they are obtained. Technology's new models promise not only improved reliability that reduces the chance of breakdown, but improved transparency that diagnoses and self-repairs breakdowns when they occur. The academy's growth, particularly in the social sciences, is based on models that are ever more liable to need rapid replacement as social change accelerates. Users need to be able to assess their reliability and validity to stop their use doing more harm than good. The model village can poison the city it was meant to enlighten, if the gap between them becomes too large, or the traffic too one-way.

Chapter 5

Prodigy to
Problem Child:
Academic Social Science

On top of providing essential inputs to 'knowledge society', universities make a unique claim to provide knowledge of society. This is the one area of study they can claim to have originated, and not just assimilated. Natural sciences long flourished outside the academy, and have never fully entered its control. Arts and humanities, similarly, were practised long before the arrival of the academy, and can still be successfully pursued outside them. Social sciences, by contrast, appeared on the scene as universities were undergoing their modern revival and expansion. Mutual interdependence was soon established, and co-evolution followed.

The academy rapidly absorbed the work of social science's 'founding fathers', and fashioned them into the mainstream disciplines of politics, sociology, economics and psychology. Subsequent proliferation of subdisciplines, carved out of the mainstream, took place wholly within it. As the twentieth century progressed, social scientists stretched academic knowledge across an ever wider spectrum of human issues, from the ultimate to the intimate, with studies extending beyond the mainstream. They probed into motives and beliefs, ideologies and the unconscious, rationality and its reversals. Social science itself became a target for study, critical theorists accusing it of assisting capitalist oppression, racism and sexism. Thinking about people can change the way that they think. This in turn ensures that social science also changes. It makes academic ideas applicable to even the most idiosyncratic human behaviour. Social science is ubiquitous, defining new problems as well as suggesting solutions, and so creating new topics for study.

Exclusivity and Ubiquity

The most obvious evidence of this growing ubiquity is the number of students and staff engaged in social disciplines. These were the chief beneficiary of postwar research and teaching expansion, in Britain and elsewhere. In the majority of the 100+ UK universities at the start of the twenty-first century, the social sciences were the largest group of subjects, contributing to the largest number of professional courses. In more than a third, over 50% of the students were reading business or social studies. These have become major faculties in academia, integral to the training of a wide range of professionals. This uptake has helped them diffuse into the school curriculum, even when this is resisted by professional bodies such as the British Sociological Association. In the UK, social studies became available as school-leaving qualifications at 16 and 18, and were even introduced into primary schools. The school leavers faced similar questions to those set fifty years earlier for graduates, asking for information on social structure plus a little theory to explain how and why this has been organised.

Popular exposure to social sciences from an early age, even for those who do not go on to specialist courses in them, substantially strengthens universities' social influence. The populace is now informed, and expects there to be experts on a wide range of economic, personal and social issues, just as much as it looks to medical doctors to give them better physical health or electronic engineers to give them better computers. Social studies promise understanding of our shared lives. Their university prospectus entries promise to combine intellectual rigour with applications to familiar problems and possible solutions. They raise expectations of increasing knowledge that will be personally as well as professionally rewarding.

Social science differentiated as it expanded in the latter half of the twentieth century, reinforcing expectations of knowing. This continuous development is part of its attraction. There's always something new on the horizon of academia that looks promising for construction, elaboration and application when the subject is the thinking, responsive human. It is never 'normal' in Kuhn's sense of working unquestioningly within paradigms (Kuhn, 1962). Only in economics is there a definable 'mainstream', and the expulsion of non-orthodox economists into neighbouring disciplines adds to their heterogeneity. Reflexive science is always engaged and adapting.

The abandonment of attempts to mirror natural science has led to a mixture of assumptions and interpretations that ensures that there is always a theory that can apply to any situation, and appeal to any client. Ubiquity is achieved through national or local variation, in contrast to natural sciences' ubiquity through universal application. Britain's version of the Enlightenment focused on the Scottish writers Hume (1711–76), Ferguson (1723–1816) and Adam Smith (1723–90). But American accounts tend to follow the French in crediting Montesquieu (1689–1755), Quesnay (1694–1774), Rousseau (1712–78), Diderot (1713–84) and D'Alembert (1727–83).

The German tradition is usually traced back to Herder (1744–1803), student of Kant and colleague of Goethe in Weimar, who rejected the optimism of the British and French Enlightenment and looked at local, organic, cultural heritage. Refugees from Nazism brought this German tradition to America and Britain in the 1930s. This 'Romanticism', emphasising the power of tradition to sustain variety in local cultures against the universal progress secured by reason, remained an important antidote to the determinism of early social science. Its contemporary survival might even be seen in the reaction of Europe's national political traditions (left and right) against the universalising designs of the EU Commission. British supporters included the poets Blake (1757–1827) and Coleridge (1772–1834), who also became a political journalist, planned a utopian community in America, and was an early explorer of the unconscious.

Another German, Weber (1864–1920), though only fully translated into English fifty years after his death, became a central figure through his analysis of the impact of capitalism. His work related its rational, disenchanted, de-mystified view to the rise of European Protestantism, with its emphasis on hard work to justify salvation, and showed how major social changes could avoid political upheaval through the legitimation of authority in different historical and cultural contexts. This extended Marx's analysis of the relation between labour markets, class consciousness and conflict, by including the way groups develop their own cultures, understandings and ways of life that are not merely determined by material circumstances. It was the major influence behind the 'interpretive turn' in the 1970s.

While economists have turned rational choice into a depiction of individual and institutional action abstracted from social context, others highlight its local variations. The Japanese managers who cover up a colleague's mistake are being no less rational, in their own eyes, than the American counterpart who tells the boss so he can beat that colleague to the next promotion. The trading practices of a European financial market would not work well in a Middle Eastern souk, but both are rational.

The romantic tradition stresses imagination, liberty, love, truth, tolerance, intuition as counterpoints or qualifiers of reason. The 'rationalising' power of neutral observation is opposed by the 'idealising' power of active human interpretation, moving the world into the mind of the observer. Constructed introspectively, knowledge can be expressed in music, poetry and art as well as scientific explanation. Romanticism survives as a rejection of the inductive, empiricist social science that was popular in Britain and North America into the second half of the twentieth century. From the collision of the two emerged a phenomenological social science that stressed the way the world was made meaningful through conceptualisation — through such central European pioneers as Lewin in Psychology, Schutz in Sociology and Hayek in economics. The human subject was assumed to be thinking, knowledgeable and imaginative, not just reactive. Even as experimental and mathematical tests were unifying the natural sciences, the social sciences were incorporating these diverse perspectives, becoming a springboard for wider application.

The Science that Builds Itself

It is easy to mock the intrusion of social science into private as well as public affairs. Ancient universities qualified professionals in theology, medicine and law. Today social sciences have moved beyond the basic disciplines of economics, psychology and sociology to offer courses in childhood and ageing, leisure and work, business and environmental management, the hidden economy, the quality of life; and specialist research projects that chase even finer gradations of wisdom, in table dancing, barber-shop singing, graffiti art or behaviour in public toilets. Through academisation, social scientists demystified and challenged the legitimacy of priest and patron, accrediting new professions to replace them. They have now emerged from the cloister as legitimate authorities on issues of everyday concern, both asking questions and providing answers.

Where people once looked to scripture for wisdom, and let their elders and betters lay down the law, they now share constructed knowledge of their selves and their relations with others. It is assumed that we know — or at least, that academics, political and business leaders and professionals know — how the economy and society work, and what condition they are in. We expect instant guidance in understanding and handling new challenges at the global level — from energy shortages and refugee crises — and insights into existential or relational crises at the personal level.

Whether seeking to mirror or setting out to modify its objects of attention, social science encourages people to look at themselves and the world around them. Initially, inspired by natural science, the main impulse was to view the social world as a system, and its participants (including the observer) as observable elements, their motives and beliefs to be inferred from their behaviour. Later, in more reflexive mode, social science added a second encouragement, for observers to consider their own role in the world. The subjective feelings they brought to it, and might empathically ascribe to others, became a relevant consideration in making observations, conducting tests and assessing their results.

Although motivated by a natural human inclination to enquire into the world — including the human's own capabilities — social science also feeds that inclination. Economics suggests we can live better and achieve more if allowed to trade through free markets using fully informed, properly calculated decisions. Politics challenges us to consider our preferences for those social and economic arrangements that require collective coordination, how these might be shaped by our class, gender, ethnicity, personal history and social position, and how they can best be satisfied when others have different preferences. Psychology encourages us to probe for the unacknowledged conditions, hidden assumptions, suppressed beliefs and genetically or experientially determined instincts that cloud and bias our judgements, even if intended as rational choices. Sociology invites us to consider human agency as constrained by internal (psychological) and external (institutional) structures, but also enabled by these structures, and constantly engaged in reconstituting or revising them in the process of obeying them.

Self-consciousness and self-reflection pre-dated the launch of social science, probably even the development of language. But social scientists encourage and augment them, by modelling a world whose inhabitants are model-builders themselves. They are not alone in characterising the tendency to model as a first step to understanding. Part of Shakespeare's timelessness rests on his recognition of this universal tendency, using metaphors to involve audiences in his plays (Bloom 1999). In everyday life, observation leads to lay theories as we peer over the garden wall. Prescriptive models, such as rational choice, may attempt to override this 'folk wisdom', pointing out choosers' logical errors and either educating them to correct these or modelling at an aggregate level where they can cancel out. Descriptive models, such as regret-minimisation or prospect theories of choice, build in the biases to characterise what people actually do and how the effects will build up. However they treat it, both types of academic theory also feed back into the lay theories, causing intentional or inadvertent modification.

Social science, applied as well as theoretical, is continuously constructing and reconstructing reality. Concepts such as capitalism, alienation, bureaucracy, competition, cognition and socialisation have been interpreted, elaborated, applied and (after simplification) incorporated into professional and everyday discourse. If knowledge is socially constructed, then so must be the social science that built it. Recognition of this, and expansion of higher education, increased the scope for social scientists to concentrate on how their own subjects had been developed. The early confidence in social physics and psychophysics has given way to acceptance that reflexivity, involved in the human studying the human, necessitates a science that cannot depend on closed-system models or controlled experimentation.

Separating the Social

After early embarrassment over 'laws' that failed to endure across time or space, most social scientists abandoned the belief that natural science methods could repeat their success in the social realm. But they have held on to the broader features of natural-scientific investigation: the belief in an identifiable social world whose workings are susceptible to study, whose findings can improve human action within the world and administration of it. That was the motive for founding the London School of Economics and Political Science at the start of the twentieth century, and it remains the motivation of most social scientists today.

The intoxicating impact of early social science owed much to its scientific label. It included both grand theories and reliable ways of collecting facts. It produced exciting insights and promised measurable ways of improving policy and practice. At the start of the twentieth century economists were still influenced by social Darwinism and the survival of the fittest, psychologists were experimenting with salivating dogs and exposed monkey brains, and sociologists had taken the concept of social engineering to its genetic roots through their involvement in eugenics. Confidence in copying the methods of the natural sciences was still alive after the two World Wars:

> Like all sciences the social sciences are experimental; they start with the facts. The basic element of their method is to look for facts and observe them. No one questions this attitude. (Duverger, 1964: 73)

By then, however, most social scientists had abandoned the claim to be conventionally scientific. They recognised the need to choose between variable-centred and account-centred, quantitative and qualitative models. The attempt to make social science relevant to everyday thought and action involves giving up the claim to be conventionally scientific. Today the focus is on all thinking humans not just an intelligentsia, insulated from the concerns of everyday life, capable of weighing up evidence from many different perspectives, as the source of impartial judgement of the human condition. Intellectuals may be able to expose interests behind the construction of knowledge, but cannot also claim to be objective themselves, cannot be insulated from the reflexivity they see as universal. If all knowledge is socially constructed, then so is social science. That has been the message of feminist, black and working class social scientists as they look at the history of their subject.

The differences between natural and social science are of context as well as method. A physicist can relax on leaving the laboratory, and ride home or kick a ball around without worrying about the laws of motion and their tendency to change. Economists can lose shirts on the stock market, psychologists become anxious and sociologists suffer from role strain. In an educated society, they have to recognise that their efforts will inspire ideas and evoke responses, thus necessitating continuous reconstruction of their disciplines. Natural scientists can control, experiment, observe and replicate to secure validity and reliability on their own terms. In the social sciences there is a reflexive, interactive relation with subjects, investigators influencing as well as influenced by those they study. The social can only be understood from the inside, not through detachment. As it responds to the accelerating changes of modern societies, social science has to keep moving.

People's desire, and ability, to give meaning to their world can frustrate attempts to control humans in experimentation. Below social science's concepts, theories and methodologies, and the increasingly sophisticated models built on them, are assumptions that are often simplistic but are usually not made public. The success of rational choice modelling in economics, and its recent extension to other disciplines, shows how an arbitrary assumption can come to underpin a major academic study. It may over-simplify people's clarity of intention, information and processing ability, but that secures its general application. In psychology and sociology, manifold assumptions support a variety of theories, securing similar ubiquity but by different means.

Accumulated, specialised social knowledge is now pyramid shaped. At the apex are Economics, Social Psychology and Sociology. Each branches into the Economics of, the Social Psychology of, the Sociology of numerous sub-disciplines. These are built into hundreds of applied courses ranging through Business to Women's Studies, Social Work to Education, Cultural to Media Studies. Between 1990 and 1995 the number of students in the UK reading social studies rose from 53,000 to 92,000. The number taking business studies rose from 20,000 to 130,000, largely through the incorporation of vocational institutions.

Ubiquity inevitably concerns government and industry, and raises questions of academic freedom as the professions and government scrutinise the content of courses. Social scientists are concerned with knowledge as power, with its uneven distribution, the prevalence of ideologies. Further, ideas applicable to humans must be applicable to those who produce them. Critical theory, for example, now the basis of a range of university subjects such as cultural, film, linguistic and women's studies, not only focuses on the taken-for-granted in social relations, but on the ideology of the social sciences themselves.

Modelling the Social

Social science is one of many attempts to understand the human condition. Revelation, speculation, tradition, imagination, political dictate, poetry and song have only recently been joined by scientific claims. All can produce convincing, if conflicting, interpretations of human behaviour. Hamlet's soliloquies confirm the hazards of participant observation, and even Frankenstein's monster engages in reflexive monitoring before turning on his scientist creator. In academia as in everyday life, modelling can range from borrowing simple metaphors to building causal structures of numerous variables. The model serves as a source of theories relating the concepts and variables involved. The sequence from making assumptions to adopting or constructing a model, and to theorising from it or testing it, is a universal way to understanding.

The metaphor-using, theorising human is impossible to model with the parsimony that enables validity to be assessed and definitions shared in natural science. Humans think. They learn from experience. Social science plays a part in that learning. That is why the controlled laboratory experiment is so risky when studying humans in social situations. The tightly defined models of particle physics enable specialists to be confident they are investigating the same phenomena or assessing the validity of the same evidence. This precision is unlikely to be attained in the social sciences without distortion and gross over-simplification. The academic temptation has been to conceptualise and then concentrate on the concepts rather than the behaviour they condense. The results have often been grand but irrelevant social scientific theories that have indeed been of less use in understanding the human than poetry or play, because the latter at least stimulate rather than dull the imagination.

The different ways of accommodating (or ignoring) feedback from their models into reality gives artists and scientists extensive choice over how to model, and similar scope on what to model. Natural scientists are clear that their models are distinct from the world, created in the specialist mind to help observe and understand that world. Social scientists cannot be so sure, because their models must include a representation of models used by individuals and groups within the model. The model in the specialist mind can be ascribed to agents within the model (as in 'rational expectations' economics), or it can make allowance for agents' seeing the world less clearly and thinking less deeply (as in 'bounded rationality' psychology). Different ways of dealing with this multi-level element in social modelling greatly multiply the variety of strategies.

A far-from-exhaustive list of models of human thinking, in just one (cognitive) area of one discipline (psychology), reveals:

Systems	**Framework**
Conceptual system	Conceptual framework
Cognitive system	Cognitive framework
Meaning system	Frame of reference
Maps	**Computer/Cognitive Models**
Mental maps	Information Processing System
Cognitive maps	Human Information Processor
Cultural maps	Central Processing Mechanism
Mental templates	Parallel Distributed Processor
Metaphors/Models	**Mind/Self**
Theoretical models	Mental representations
Guiding metaphors	Mental set
Organisational metaphors	Schema
Conceptual models	Eidos
	Generalised other
Structures	Social self
Mental construct	
Cognitive structures	
Perceptual structures	
Data structures	
Personal constructs	

Many, especially non-specialist, readers of the literature see little difference among these characterisations, and argue that different terms have been applied to what is essentially the same thing. Social science's progress, in terms of articles published if not concepts advanced, often relies on distinguishing concepts once viewed as interchangeable. Distinctions between stocks and flows, being in-itself and for-itself, use value and exchange value, sponsored and contest systems — even epistemology and ontology, or single- and double-loop learning — can, once grasped, substantially change our understanding of ourselves and our world. Those between happiness and pleasure, understanding and explanation, constitutive and retributive justice, ability and aptitude are more subtle, but no less profound in their personal and system implications. There is, however, need for a device to stop valuable concept-splitting turning into academic hair-splitting. Models provide such a device.

The representations in the scheme above fall into a smaller number of categories, each suggesting a general model within which individual terms and concepts can be situated and compared. The overlaps between seemingly separate terms and concepts can then be identified, as can differences between some that are superficially similar. Models have kept in check the drawers of distinctions with a countervailing source of progress — spotting commonalities or convergences between ideas that might have been overlooked, or even deliberately disguised, by authors and approaches keen to advertise their thinking as new.

As models gain influence, their underlying assumptions move beyond question, any debate being over the appropriateness of the model's application rather than the appropriateness of the model itself. The theory of free trade, whose (theoretically) demonstrated welfare benefits have induced a global abandonment of protective barriers in pursuit of economic growth, still rests on assumptions of perfect competition, free flow of information, full employment and an absence of economies of scale, none of which is obviously applicable to present global conditions.

Theorists whose work is equated with others' in this way often complain that the unifying model has reduced their square peg to sawdust in the process of fitting it into the round hole. Many rough edges must certainly be sawn off when recasting Marx's economics into a rational choice framework, demonstrating that the same 'logistic growth' curve governs the spread of automobile use and the release dates of Fellini's films, or shrinking Sheldrake's 'morphogenetic field' into an outmoded vitalist framework. Those defending the distinctness of their own approach react especially strongly against its presentation as a 'special case' of some less rarefied and more widely applicable approach. But translation into a model whose assumptions are explicit and terms precisely defined is often the only way to restart any dialogue across subject boundaries. Even if the opening exchanges are mainly of writs for misrepresentation, they often give way to more civilised argument, ranking above the studied silence that went before.

Similar lists could be constructed from any social science, steadily lengthening as changed conditions or methods of analysis prompt new accounts without dethroning the old. Mercantilism, phrenology, alchemy and positivism were convincing in their day. So were more recent models such as the Labour Theory of Value, g factor intelligence, and universal stages of social development or economic growth. Each was of its time and place, but each will have echoes at a later time, leading subsequent scholars to reinvoke or reinvent them. Once model-building by ordinary individuals runs alongside, and interacts with, model-building by special investigators, the social world and ideas about it start changing at an accelerating pace. Researchers, interacting with their subjects, cannot refer to an unchanged model for long without risking redundancy. To Kuhn (1962), normal science consists of exploiting the insights from models until the returns diminish or some new model becomes more promising. In the social sciences however the speed of change in modelling is not just a sign of disciplines in their adolescence, frequently ascending and descending, but of the capacity of humans to change their world, and of the interaction between this common sense and the academic knowledge it both reflects and influences.

After modelling how the mind works, social sciences have been similarly inventive — and prone to disagreement — in modelling the way humans behave. In all cases the models are only approximations to an assumed reality. The assumptions will reflect conflicting political views. They form the focus of specialist academic communities. They yield knowledge that is likely to be compounded and applied. They account for questions asked, what is included and excluded, even though they are liable to remain implicit once outside the community that used them as their focus of attention.

Reflexivity and the Expectation of Knowing

The reflexive relation between social scientists and their subjects also makes it easy to slip between model and reality. Applications of social science are always at risk of reification. Concepts such as productivity, rationalisation, race, class and sex enter both popular and academic discourse as real rather than models. The confusion can be liberating or stifling. Models can help make sense of the everyday, or be confused with it, helping engagement with the world or causing painful collisions with it.

The range of assumptions in social science modelling is wide. The human in Marxist economics thinks and acts in line with class interests. Contemporary neoclassical economists assume that humans maximise their material wellbeing subject to budgetary constraints. Sociologists assume that humans play roles in a human drama written for them, while others assume that individuals construct their own social reality. Elsewhere in academia some psychologists insist on experimental controls that eliminate thinking, in order to measure the effects of stimuli upon responses, while others focus on thinking as the determinant of behaviour. The implications of these choices engage a few social theorists. At the other end of the supply chain, knowledge professionals and lay users may not even realise that the various bases (or biases) account for the results obtained.

The gene, the atom, the black hole and most other phenomena observed or theorised by natural science are beyond everyday experience, and not changed by being studied. In contrast, social sciences deal with the thinking and acting, buying and selling, giving and taking, loving and hating that are staples of everyday experience. The more time, inclination and ability humans have to reflect on that experience, the more likely they are to be open to academic ideas. By driving the expansion of higher education, social science created the appetite for its insights that could justify, and continue, that expansion. Whereas the terms and symbols used in natural-science models tend to be analogues of real-world phenomena, those of social science are mostly invented categories. Atoms, molecules, cells and fields tend to be observable, measurable and manipulable. Class consciousness, peer pressure, the labour supply curve and achievement motivation are constructs, abstracted and aggregated from specific cases or posited in the absence of any observable case.

Interpretive social science is unlimited in scope compared with the empiricism it displaced. It can reflect on any human concern using insights from social scientific theory plus any available facts and figures. This potential of the interpretive can be seen in the titles of Clawson's (1998) list of bestselling social science titles. This includes *The Lonely Crowd, Tally's Corner, The Pursuit of Loneliness, The Fall of Public Man, Blaming the Victim, Habits of the Heart, Worlds of Pain, Intimate Strangers, Beyond the Melting Pot* and *The Hidden Inju-*

ries of Class. Few readers would fail to find something of personal interest.

Reflexivity creates a more fluid relation between scientist and subject than the direct link of natural science to technology. Foucault's (1972) archaeological and genealogical approaches have exposed the way that characterisations and explanations of social phenomena can change radically over time. The history of ideas and practices can be reconstructed to challenge taken-for-granted, contemporary beliefs. 'Archaeology' in a university library also reveals how social scientists have reinterpreted their subjects as the world they study changes.

Just as natural science asserted, and spread, a belief in figuring and reconfiguring the natural world around us, social science sows the expectation that we can, through our own efforts, understand and improve the social world. Its theoretical core enables academic peers, professionals and laity to question, explain, relate, compare, validate knowledge. Social disciplines' prominence in university prospectuses reinforced the idea of an explicable world in a language that is already becoming familiar in media and everyday discourse. This is why a few academics concentrate on obscure and conflicting models of the human condition, and most introductory texts now include reference to methodology, even if the logic is then ignored.

Far from being undermined, academic social science's authority was enhanced by the loss of 'objectivity'. If a study's conclusions can be established purely by hypothesis, experiment, observation and interpretation, there is little need to confine it to the academy. Even though universities' resources and reputations may help them to concentrate research, outsiders can still comment and contribute, if they follow approved procedures for investigation and reporting. But once science becomes a matter of judgement — with decisive experimental tests not being possible, or open to differing interpretations — authentication depends on the judgement of experts. Universities' concentration of these, in peer-reviewing networks, gives them a central role in identifying fact and conferring validity on opinion.

Those who identified the interpretive turn could also draw comfort from an apparently similar shifting of ground in the natural sciences. These lost their classical certainty with the passage from Newtonian mechanics into Einsteinian relativity, and the 'quantum' recognition of key aspects of the natural world as observer-dependent. Social science's classical, positivist phase was much shorter, its early efforts at deduction and empirical verification quickly colliding with the open-system nature of the world. Researchers' inescapable involvement, and people's ability to learn from their ideas and react to their policies, annuls straightforward cause-effect relations and ensures social systems' unpredictable development through time. By the 1970s, translations of Husserl, Schutz and others had reached British departments, and refugees from Nazi persecution were reinforcing the interpretive turn in America, highlighting the importance of the meanings given to events. There were costs and benefits. Scientism was authoritative. Unfettered interpretation spread the influence of social science, but reinforced hostility from government and professional associations to the insertion of what looked like speculation under the label of science into the training of teachers and social workers.

Academisation and rising expectations of knowing in educated populations are mutually reinforcing. A continual interaction between ordinary people's and social scientists' views of the world is acknowledged in the 'double hermeneutic' coined by Anthony Giddens — who even tried to translate it into a political 'Third Way' between neo-liberalism's rampant individualism and socialism's top-down structure. Social understanding is no longer confined to an elite. Few may speak the language of rational choice, or cognition, or symbolic interactionism; but many discuss markets, the way we think, the roles we play, the complexities of race, class and sex.

Because of its success in keeping control of knowledge, academised social science also tilts the balance of power. Academic language excludes ordinary subjects from the debate, and the switch from direct to model-based observation can even displace them as objects of study. Even if more than ever now crowd into its lecture theatres, academic actors have stripped their performances of audience participation. Outside academia the language used and concepts employed radiate through school lessons, broadcasting, journalism and popular culture. Social science spreads theoretical knowledge into common sense. It offers to explain the workings of international trade, the determinants of perception, the construction of sexism, the relation between natural science and technology, the differences between philosophy and ideology, and probes into its own prejudices. Retention of the authority of academic scrutiny and internal validation shields it from the charge that it is just wrapping academic buzzwords around commonsense ideas.

However, thinking humans interpret ideas and evidence as they are received. An increasingly educated public adapts and uses social scientific insights, often without realising their origin. Social science increasingly produces the foresight and hindsight through which the world is understood. Humans think about their world from the intimate to the global. Social scientists contribute, and respond to the consequences of their own contributions as they build an archive now accessible worldwide.

Thus social science has matched the impact of natural science, but in a more subtle and ultimately fundamental way. Science-based technology and industry transforms the world through obvious material innovation: the telephone, car, computer, internet, aircraft, antibiotics. Social science transforms the world invisibly, sometimes insidiously, by changing the way we view and approach it, even shaping our perception and use of the new technologies. The quest to understand how experts have come to analyse the world, and then understand how ordinary people's changed understanding further changes the world, draws students onto its courses, academics to the media and policy makers to the latest buzzwords.

Conclusion: Teaching Double Vision

Academised natural sciences and arts are reflections on material or human realities that would still exist if reflection stopped. They comprise independent worlds — where things exist and people coexist — that provide a reality check for the conclusions drawn from their study. In contrast, social science enjoys (and exploits) the power to create and redefine its subject of study. Social phenomena can be constituted or changed by the process of analysis, so cannot provide an independent check on that analysis. While academic natural science exploited the move from retrieved to revealed knowledge, academic social science opened up the possibility of invented knowledge. It underwrote universities' expansion by opening up unlimited potential for new ideas, and for creating demand to absorb that new supply.

The academisation of the social sciences within the twentieth century, coinciding with the expansion of higher education, made them the major source of knowledge of the human condition and of applications for its improvement. They have vastly expanded their influence on an increasingly educated, professionalised society by amplifying the expectation of knowing. In the very act of capturing and systematising the creation and validation of knowledge, the academy unleashed changes that stripped away the 'objective' basis on which creation and validation of that knowledge had previously rested. But this ensures that, even as it engaged in the social world as a supposedly equal partner, the academy retained its autonomy and enhanced its validation role.

Social disciplines' unique selling point, ensuring a comparable growth in demand, was the promise of release from constraint — of community, religion, superstition, political repression or commercial mismanagement. Social science could throw off the world's attitudinal and organisational constraints, in the way that natural science had rolled back the world's natural resource constraints. The rational choice model, especially as developed in economics, focused attention on human choice according to a maximising calculus. The switch in social psychology from studying the effects of stimuli on individual behaviour to those arising from group interaction had an immediate impact on studies of human relations, leadership and management. Risk, shame, guilt, love and choice became legitimate and enlightening targets for enquiry. An interpretive turn from the last quarter of the twentieth century quickened their ascent.

Chapter 6

Applying Commodified Knowledge

As fast as academia tightens its grip on the creation of knowledge, applications of that knowledge move further away from it. Higher education's reach relentlessly broadens, absorbing previously non-academic subject areas. But in the process, its grasp is often made weaker. Once validated by the academy, knowledge and its holders swiftly move beyond it, to institutions it can only loosely influence and applications it does not directly monitor. Control over who gets to produce, validate and disseminate knowledge has kept universities internally coherent during the dramatic growth in their research and teaching output. But a tighter core means a looser periphery. The rising social impact of that output reflects, and reinforces, an ever greater threat to the academy's retention of external control.

The variety in the attempts to produce a science of the social is enhanced by its being embedded in time and place. From the viewpoint of the twenty-first century, Adam Smith seems to contradict himself over the benefits of self-interest. Auguste Comte now seems deluded, Sigmund Freud sexist, Karl Marx dogmatic, Herbert Spencer eugenicist, William McDougall patronising. Even their views selected as relevant today have to be interpreted. The more embarrassing is archived or left untranslated. Today both social change and the redundancy of models of it are accelerating.

This acceleration, combined with the longer lifetimes and careers of academic social scientists, means that knowledge acquired in as little as three years within the academy walls may now enjoy 30–40 years' application outside it, the holders often having no further contact with their alma mater except for alumni reunions and donation appeals. Longer production lines in private enterprise, and command lines in public bureaucracies, mean that knowledge released from the academy must go through ever more interpretation, simplification, recombination and repackaging before it finally emerges as an economic or social product. On both dimensions, universities' escalating power over the production of knowledge risks being compromised by diminishing power over its distribution, re-trading, interpretation and application.

Reflexivity's Risks and Rewards

The academic absorption of social science's foundations, and accommodation of its applications, was largely complete by the end of the twentieth century. The amateur was excluded, from theory and application. Referencing and conversation were internalised. The accumulation of knowledge legitimated not only the academic, but also the professional in public and private sectors, while changing lay perceptions of humanity's place in the social world. Retrieved knowledge was replaced by knowledge constructed within secure, specialist academic communities, claiming freedom from external interference. Professional associations such as the British Psychological Society, British Sociological Association, Royal Economic Society, and their European and American equivalents, defined their subjects and imposed norms of academic behaviour.

The academisation of social science coincided with recognition that a new social order was needed. Beatrice and Sidney Webb, co-founders of the London School of Economics, at the start of the twentieth century were active in London local government and influential social reformers. Academia provided a secure base for studying economy, society and the individual, the potentially subversive issues of the distribution of wealth and power across race, class and sex, and how these related to individuals' understanding of their lives. But by the end of the century it was accepted that where natural science was concerned with a world that could be observed through microscope or telescope and could be controlled for experimentation, reflexive, interpretive social sciences studying the relation between individual and society, action and structure had to bridge the 'micro-macro' divide. Economists who trace national output, employment and inflation to rational action by individuals and firms, clash with their Keynesian, Marxist and institutionalist colleagues, who analyse collective effects for which individual choice is effect rather than cause. Social psychology belies its unifying ambition by splitting into sociological and psychological factions. Social theory seeks distance from sociology when it sees this becoming too individualist and reductionist, dissolving the society it claims to study.

Each social science has a variety of assumptions, models, theories and methods that resolve the problem in contrasting ways. It can be treated as the specific concern of philosophers of social science, dealing with ontology (what is out there to study), epistemology (how we can know about what is there) and methodology (how we can go about finding out what is there). But it can also be dismissed as itself set-up by philosophers and social scientists using different interpretations of science, the mind and the way humans learn and use language (see, for example, Button et al., 1995). Or it can be bypassed by arbitrarily modelling human activity. Economists' 'general equilibrium theory', a century in the making, shows how maximising individuals' coordination solely by free markets can generate an optimal allocation of resources which maximises total income and eliminates involuntary unemployment. But its requirement for (among other conditions) full information, instantaneous price adjustment, present and futures markets for everything and no economies of scale leaves many outside this 'neoclassical' citadel wondering why its occupants have taken refuge in such an architectural curiosity.

Many efforts have been made to get between individual action and collective outcome by modelling a dynamic interaction between the two. Examples are Giddens' structuration theory, Bourdieu's reflexive sociology and Habermas' communicative action — linking (respectively) agency and structure, habitus and field, life-world and system. These theories define individual understanding by reference to rules generated in social institutions. They avoid a lapse into idealism, reducing structure to agency, by assuming an underlying reality that exists independently of conceptions of it, and may not be directly observable. A more arbitrary solution is to ignore the problem, observing behaviour and collecting 'facts' in search of understandings that fit and solutions that work, regardless of any theoretical grounding. Such pragmatism is rarely admitted or supported by those at the frontiers of knowledge, who see their mission as producing something deeper. But lower down the knowledge chain, it is what the majority of social scientists engage in as they reify concepts, apply theoretical insights, collect data and compound original knowledge in the course of teaching and professional preparation.

None of these approaches have avoided the criticism that social science has been biased. Feminists have had a long and unfinished struggle not just to secure equal opportunities, but to expose sexism within social science itself. In the nineteenth century Marshall and Freud were overtly patriarchal, and Durkheim blamed female fatalism for producing lower suicide rates when on his theory they should have been higher. But feminist criticism has not stopped gender inequality in the payrolls and practices of institutions, including those of higher education. Similarly, social class and racial bias have been repeatedly exposed. Social scientists cannot disengage from their subjects.

The interactive relation between social scientist and subject can be seen in the coming and going of ideas. The corporate state is a powerful idea in the 1970s but outdated by the 1990s. Social psychologists develop self-concept theory in the 1960s. It was introduced into teaching and parenting in the 1970s, but then becomes one of many explanations for motivation used by professionals as replications reveal flaws. Over time an educated population itself begins to see the world through increasingly specialised concepts developed in academia. The social science of Wallas or Hobhouse as the London School of Economics was established is now unconvincing in its generality. But whereas natural scientists can definitively reject ideas that are empirically or logically untenable — so that none now clings to belief in phlogiston, the ether or the geocentric universe — social sciences have no equivalent to this natural science stock clearance or deposit into a separate History of Science.

This reluctance to bury the redundant, criticise the outdated and warn against applying the dubious is part of the insecurity of social scientists as they have been rapidly established. The ambitious move into line. Senior academics keep one eye on their departments' reputations. The radical is accommodated. But criticism across specialisms and along the value chains is inhibited. Applications often horrify those who initially floated the ideas that produced them. But there will always be academics sufficiently confident to publish and advise on the growth boost to be expected from a currency devaluation or the profitable pricing of a privatised railway, through to the need to ensure that young children are never deprived of their mother's company. People and politicians who act in good faith on such advice face the wrath of their family members or cabinet colleagues. Those who served it up merely retreat to recalibrate their model, and live to advise another day.

The Danger in Academic Knowledge

All academic social scientists from basic producers of theory to retailers engage in professional and vocational training. All produce knowledge, but influence tends to flow from basic to applied, not only because they bring new perspectives to old problems, but because they lend established academic authority to more recently developed applications. But models are built from defined variables or explicit accounts within specified boundaries. The scope for application is restricted by that definition. Their authority within academia simultaneously proscribes other perceptions. They have to convince peers to be published. But they can then be wholesaled in academia to business and management, anxiety and stress, culture and media in the training of professionals. Then they can influence everyday behaviour and thought, often after being stripped of assumptions, left on reading lists and taken out of context.

The dominant figure in early English social psychology had been William McDougall (1871–1938), co-founder of the British Psychological Association and professor of psychology in London and Oxford, where he tutored Cyril Burt. McDougall was editor of the British Journal of Psychology for 34 years to 1938. His *Introduction to Social Psychology* was written to provide a psychological basis for the social sciences. First published in 1908, it reached its 31st edition in 1963, and remained on the reading list for the Postgraduate Certificate in Education at London's Institute of Education into the late 1960s. It described instincts as the basis from which the character and will of individuals and nations are gradually developed. Students had to reconcile this with the radically different ideas reaching them from sociology and somehow use it in their teaching.

When initial teacher training was extended to a three-year course, the Sociology of Education became a key component in the 1970s. Exciting ideas were rapidly adopted and adapted, particularly over the role of language in consolidating the division between home and school. The conclusion that school cannot compensate for society contained a radical message for teachers. If children were expected to drop their 'deprived' home culture at the school gate, because 'parents are inadequate in both the moral and skill orders they transmit' (Bernstein, 1970: 113), the subject-centred school curriculum needed reforming. Bernstein later admitted that he unintentionally produced this unfortunate view (1996: 114). But by then teacher training already included the idea that education had to be negotiated, and children given the opportunity to impose their own meanings on the school curriculum (Esland, 1971).

The Auld Report (1976) into the consequences of this thinking at one troubled London school coincided with Inner London Education Authority surveys showing low standards of literacy and numeracy, particularly among deprived groups. The Great Debate opened by the Labour government in 1976 was the start of a reaction against this academic view of education as negotiation, and the recognition that children — of all backgrounds — needed literacy and numeracy before they could negotiate. By the 1990s there was growing debate over whether teacher education, increasingly conducted in schools, could still be justified as a university subject. Yet Education faculties are a major part of most universities. De-skilling of the profession may be a frequent lament of its practitioners, but de-academisation is not on the agenda.

With typical prescience, Barbara Wootton had responded to the Younghusband Report (1959) on social work by challenging the assumption that social science could provide the 'good understanding of human needs, motivation and behaviour' that practitioners needed (Wootton, 1959). She thought that Shakespeare might have been a better guide. That judgement was enthusiastically echoed forty years later by Bloom (1999), but not by the rapidly growing ranks of professional social scientists. By the mid-1970s there was concern both in government and in academic departments of Sociology over the spread of superficial social science in teacher training. Claims were being made that teachers should be trained in psychology and sociology rather than studying subjects to be taught in schools (Price, 1966). Economics was demanding inclusion, perhaps anticipating the marketisation of education, with schools competing for pupils and resources and head teachers running them with one eye on the budget.

Bernstein's misfortune was to have an original idea immediately taken up by politicians and professionals, before the requisite time for checks on its accuracy and an impact assessment of strategy changes it might inspire. His ideas pushed against an unexpectedly open door. In other instances the door stays closed, giving academics more time to refine and package their novel thinking. But the social consequences can be just as serious when a shift in professional or political need gives their prescriptions sudden currency. Monetarist theories of inflation lay quietly on the academic shelves until the stagflation of the 1970s. Then the abandonment of apparently failed 'Keynesian' routes to full employment with stable prices left governments casting round for a new approach, which they found in the by-now well documented proposition that inflation was curable by restraining the growth of the money supply. The more sophisticated academic 'monetarists' had already warned that the seemingly firm link between money-supply growth and price growth might break down (through changes in agents' behaviour) if the first were explicitly used to control the second. They had also made clear that while monetary contraction would affect only inflation in the long run, it could severely reduce output and employment in the short run if price-setters did not immediately adapt to the new regime. But these warning notes rarely reached the ears of the political monetarists now surrounding Margaret Thatcher and Ronald Reagan, whose nation-sized 'monetarist' experiments inflicted deep, de-industrialising recessions that later rebounded into further inflationary booms. The evolutionary process of academic variation and political selection makes the breakthrough moment uncertain; but few things match the power — for good or ill — of an idea whose time has come.

New ideas can have a practical impact even if their academic vogue is brief. For example, *Schooling in Capitalist America* (Bowles and Gintis, 1976) claimed that schools served mainly to produce a disciplined workforce. This American analysis was immediately inserted into British teacher-training literature. Criticism mounted of the assumption that the ideology of teachers corresponded with the norms of capitalism, and that schools were effective in their indoctrination, especially as worse problems were identified in the alternatives to capitalism. Within ten years, the originators had retracted (Bowles and Gintis, 1986). But their change of heart did not have the instant and widespread appeal of their original suggestion. Whether intentionally or not, tutors familiar with ideas of behaviour modification, innate ability or industrial-age constraints on family life were misleading students on a brief course sandwiched into a mainly practical training. New ideas took on the same intoxicating quality as new beers, resulting in the same sometimes comic, sometimes tragic mis-steps by those who drank too deeply. Rosenthal and Jacobsen's *Pygmalion in the Classroom* (1968) showed how American children benefited from raised teacher expectations. The impact in Britain on teacher training was immediate. Raising the self-image of children became a priority, even though the slipshod design of the original research and the failure of replications to get similar results was soon exposed (Elashoff and Snow, 1971).

Rosenthal was an academic psychologist, Jacobsen a school administrator. Smiling and flattering to raise attainment was an attractive idea. Its academic demolition took less than three years. However, few teachers read the *American Educational Research Journal* in which this was published. The self-fulfilling prophecy entered the folklore of teaching. It became popular in the 1960s at the height of the progressive primary education movement in Britain. It was inserted into teacher training and teaching, particularly through two popular books, *How Children Fail* and *How Children Learn*, stressing that children wanted to learn, but experienced school as a prison (Holt, 1965a and 1965b). In Holt's self-concept theory, there was a simple answer to why children fail: 'Because adults treated them as if it were so' (Holt, 1965a: 80).

Holt's views became the subject of withering academic criticism (Hare, 1985). But they and the 'Pygmalion' research reinforced the move away from the traditional concentration on literacy and numeracy in primary schools. In the Inner London Education Authority it led to attempts to ban record-keeping in primary schools to ensure that no adverse evidence was passed on with the risk of teachers lowering their expectations. This deflected attention from the quality of teaching, assessment of attainment, the content of the curriculum and the management of schools. Stone (1981) also pointed out that while teachers were trying to compensate black children for their low self-concept, black parents were using supplementary schools to compensate for inadequate teaching in the mainstream.

The extent to which sociology in particular penetrated the professional training of teachers was remarkable, given the little time available on one-year post-graduate and even on four-year Bachelor of Education (BEd) degrees that had to include teaching practice, method courses and, in the latter, subject courses. Such inclusion confirmed the power of social science. The University of London BEd examinations for 1979 contained such questions as 'Evaluate ethnomethodology's claim to provide an analysis of the routine performances whereby members' competencies are achieved'; 'Discuss the Freudian view that religious belief can be explained in non-religious terms as a product of the unconscious'; and 'Discuss Hume's criticism of the Teleological Argument'. Within five years the government had intervened to ensure that students concentrated on subjects they would teach in school and on how to teach them, rather than skate across the surface of social science. A national curriculum was launched to ensure that teachers concentrated on the basic skills. Concern shifted from whether teachers could tell their ethnomethodology from their ethnocentrism to whether they had basic qualifications in maths and English, before attempting to pass these on to those they taught.

Even when aware of them, those administering professional courses did not attempt to overcome contradictions among social sciences they conveyed. Such reconciliation would have been unprofessional, even within the same institute. Minds were regarded as stronger for being able to contain contradictory assumptions. So ideas could stay alive in a multidisciplinary course even when rejected generations before in the subject of origin. There might even be rewards in fusing immiscible concepts, or knowingly departing from original texts. It is exhilarating both to produce new ideas for specialist academic peers and to apply these to practice.

The Power of Loose Models

The need to establish the credibility of academic social science, organise it on a large scale and stop its controversies turning into conflicts has meant a tightening of discipline on knowledge production, validation and application. Pre-academic nineteenth-century attempts to identify stages or laws of social development now seem excessively speculative. Comte's law of three stages, Marx's historical materialism, Spencer's evolutionary model of social change, and perceived shifts from community to association or from mechanical to organic solidarity are now viewed as over-generalised, over-simplified and even dogmatic. Comtemporary examples such as pre-modernity, simple modernity and reflexive modernity are still speculative; but they at least have the reinforcement of references to accumulated work on the same themes, itself referenced to published work that won peer approval.

Academic communities are organised to control entry, promotion, appointments, publication, conference and reference. Their membership can be defined by a particular subject of study, or a particular perspective and methodology applicable to a variety of subjects. Entry is achieved through long education, qualification and gradual promotion, success in which depends on approval of seniors. Success means learning what behaviour and attitudes are acceptable, how far to generalise, which subjects are taboo or politically sensitive, which networks to join, which areas of interest are most likely to yield results and funds for further research. Academia's formal rule book is shorter than that of most professions only because the most telling constraints are exercised informally, through institutional pedigree and peer appraisal. This discipline allows academics, like other professionals, to strengthen their market position, by limiting the numbers qualified to practise and encouraging demand for their services from governments, citizens and businesses.

Strong discipline also limits the variety of thinking and modelling within an academic community. But variety is maintained within social science as a whole by the proliferation of communities, and discipline by professional associations. The British Psychological Society (BPS) approves courses and accredits psychologists to practise as BPS members. The British Sociological Association tried to exclude 'amateurs' as the subject was academised in the 1960s, and then settled for a 'teachers section' hoping that would identify a professional core. However, this coincided with the subject entering technical and teacher training colleges and then schools, often staffed by the unqualified. This led not only to acrimony but problems over who was to be accepted as a teacher. All professional associations also deal with ethical issues, but only in Psychology does this carry the weight which comes from controlling entry to professional practices. But above all, they have become highly specialised in a short time period.

The notion of convergence and reunification of disciplines, still alive in natural science, is thus firmly off the social science agenda. Half a century ago, McDougall was not unusual in assuming that the social sciences would converge after their unfortunate years apart. To him, all approaches to human society had come to rest on individual behaviour, so agreement on a model for that behaviour would unify the many disciplines built on it. Towards the end of the century there were still hopes that cognitive or evolutionary psychology, the interpretive turn in anthropology and sociology, even economists' rational choice theory could provide a new basis for general theory. Dahrendorf (1995b) still anticipated a cure for excessive specialisation through the development of cross-disciplines such as political economy, economic history and social anthropology. But these have themselves become highly specialised. Different disciplines compete to provide alternative concepts, categories and catchphrases with which to comprehend what happens around us and to us. Academics may appear to cut through the complexities of the world, but only by using incompatible models based on many contrasting assumptions.

Beyond academia, and increasingly within it, knowledge is adopted and adapted for popularity. Among the bestselling management writers, Stephen Covey's *Seven Habits of Highly Effective People* (1989) is a mixture of anecdote, analysis and academic referencing that has sold over 5 million copies. Its thinking is refined and taught at the Covey Leadership Centre, just as the Anthony Robbins Foundation builds on the founder's *Awake the Giant Within* (1992). These successful entrepreneurs combine flair and fervour with techniques for instant motivation. The concepts they use are traceable to academic psychology, but the subjects covered and the language used are evangelical rather than academic. Appealing concerns for empowerment, prioritising, total quality, synergy and unleashing personal power are made irresistible by the assurance of science, however far this has been stretched from the purpose and context in which it first appeared.

Popular books that paraphrase serious research are often derided by academics. Yet they influence academic ideas as well as giving them publicity. Edward de Bono's widely sold paperbacks on lateral thinking were a contribution to Psychology's switch from behaviourism to cognition. Benjamin Spock was an antidote to extremes in the academic study of child development from the 1960s to the 1990s. The academisation of knowledge promotes the feeling that we should know and opens the way for popular works that meet that demand and in turn necessitate new academic thinking. Beyond the academic are books, courses and lectures that offer alternative and guaranteed recipes for success. You can change your life in seven days, triple your income in three months and make yourself futurewise. There are over 100 titles in the Sheldon Press series Overcoming Popular Problems, giving sensible advice on common worries such as the blues, stress and irritable bowels.

While there is always plenty of choice on bringing up baby, social science's changing perceptions mean it is safest to obtain one recently written. Putting yesterday's advice into practice may now invite prosecution for cruelty. Yet such advice is always valued at the time; and each publication, from the academic to the popular, increases demand even if it shows up the errors in what went before. The Institutes for the Achievement of Human Potential in Philadelphia ran seven-day courses on How to Multiply Your Baby's Intelligence. The claim was that every child has, at birth, more potential intelligence than Leonardo da Vinci ever used (Doman et al ., 1994). With that encouraging prospect, young mothers using Doman methods had taught their babies to read in English and in two or three other languages, and maths at a rate that left them agog. These sources flourish because people now expect to know. Academics have raised expectations, but tend to leave it to others to publish for those most affected.

This delegation means that the 'scientific' sequence of theory, assumptions, model, theory-check is frequently short-circuited. Assumptions can be left implicit, concealing the contradictions that their explication might reveal. Models can be built without underlying theory (as with economists' vector-auto-regression models, which often forecast no less reliably than those that are theory-based), and can be debated and 'calibrated' without effort to relate them back to the world. The computer was adopted as a model for studying cognition with scant consideration for the assumption that a programmed machine, enacting complex processes from simple instructions, was an appropriate source for theorising about the human. Neoclassical economic models were based on the assumption that individuals act rationally on the basis of all available information. Functionalist theory was based on a model of society as organism, on the assumption that individuals played parts enabling societies to work, thus ignoring their capacity to think and act to change their world.

It is the wealth of assumptions that are most likely to be missing in publication. Metaphors can be mixed, models reduced to little more than similes, theories left contradictory. Structuralism a century ago used an atomic model, assuming perception to ascend from simple to complex. Gestalt theories adopted a holistic model that assumed the whole to be more than the sum of the parts. Cognitive theory followed, returning to the nineteenh century assumptions, but using the experimental methods of the twentieth. Those radical and rapid changes are now built into the social scientific canon. Even the absurd of yesterday is reinterpreted, placed in a modern context and published as another step in the progress of social science.

However, a high price has often been paid for generalisation from loosely defined models such as historical materialism, the superego, knowledge as control. Similar balance sheets will be presented for globalisation, achievement motivation, the Third Way. The chances of judgement being fully informed decline with the distance between producers and users of academic knowledge. Yet these generalised models are the most likely to be relevant for application, and of interest outside the small circle of originators. Scientists are thus perpetually at risk of seeing their most casually floated, least formalised models becoming the ones that capture public imagination, and are most forcibly served on that public by those spreading knowledge down the chain. Dawkins' suggestion of 'memes' as cultural complements to genes, Jung's theory of personality types (and their Myers-Briggs formulation), and the 'Laffer Curve', showing that tax cuts could increase public revenue, are among the products of back-of-envelope models that caught the public imagination, and took on an extracurricular life of their own. Precision can threaten generalisability, so loose models yield most insights. Precisely because they package ideas for easier inspection, and weave stories around them for easier digestion, models let the waiters escape the watchful eye of the chef and amplify the academic problem of control.

Conclusion: Dividing and Ruling

The co-existence of contrasting, specialist assumptions, models and theories means that there can be little accumulation of knowledge between Economics and Sociology, between the many approaches in social Psychology, between the many specialisms within each subject and across their many applications. Compounding knowledge should ideally start with checking ontological and epistemological compatibility. In practice, the majority ignore the problems or adopt a naive realism that enables them to get on with the application of knowledge. However, disagreements over fundamental assumptions inevitably lead to palace revolutions, paradigm shifts, iconoclasm. Social science and the social world interact and hence are always being changed.

Despite this, social science has been pervasive in its influence. If it cannot show how to control economies, solve disputes with our neighbours, or explain the persistence of social inequality, it can at least offer insights and possible ways to cope. Accumulating data and advancing technique hold open the hope that, next time, the recommended policy action will work, and the forecast be fulfilled. Academic wholesalers and retailers encourage those ambitions. If there are ecological economists, stress counsellors and feminist sociologists, they will create concern for the environment, feelings that we are under strain, and awareness of women's subordination. Academics engage with the issues they help to identify, and use their authority to clarify what is in our world and in our minds.

Reflexivity, allied to the academy's knowledge monopoly, helps social science co-opt its critics. Feminists can now be found in the departments they vigorously criticise. Critical theorists attack their colleagues for supporting an established order of which they themselves are members. Postmodernist sociologists condemn their own discipline as a legacy of flawed modernity, echoing the fabled philosophers who spent a lifetime disproving the possibility of philosophy. Mainstream economists who preach the ineffectiveness of economic policy still welcome politicians' call to be their economic advisers. Disciplines' self-criticism becomes another source of specialisation, as feminists, critical theorists, postmodernists organise their own growth areas in academia and benefit from the process.

The variegated products of academic enterprise take physical (and, increasingly, cyberspatial) form in thousands of journals, ranging from pure theory to applications from aeronautics to zookeeping. This is referenced knowledge, linking the new to what is already established and validated. It locates the authors, selects the peer group who will approve its publication, and ensures that it is written in an academically acceptable language and format. Academisation of professions, arts and crafts means that their quality becomes an academic responsibility. So peer review and referencing extend into the accreditation of accountants and lawyers, doctors and nurses, social workers and teachers, and to the applications, policies and practices in which they engage.

Social science emerges as beguiling but dangerous. When Hayek received his Nobel prize in 1974 he spoke of the need for social scientists to be gardeners rather than craftsmen (Hayek, 1974). They should cultivate rather than shape. The claim to be scientific had led economists to forget that they deal with unobservable and unmeasurable factors. It was a warning for all social scientists as their influence spread, within and beyond academia. People can be enlightened and informed. They will demand to be, once possessed of a basic education and the resources required to pay for more of it. By feeding ideas to them, social scientists may complicate what they study. Social processes can be characterised, but their consequences cannot be predicted or controlled.

Chapter 7

The Business of Knowledge

Most universities must deal increasingly with private business as a source of funds, equipment and sponsored students, as well as of remunerative intellectual puzzles. But few like being compared with private businesses, and there is grumbling in the ranks at any vice-chancellor who covets the role of chief executive. As a professor at Warwick University Ltd (Thompson 1971), one of the authors of this book listened to many criticisms of the direction in which vice-chancellor Jack Butterworth had steered it. Too much business-driven research and teaching risks the generation and transmission of knowledge as a tradeable product, rather than a good thing in itself. Commercial motivation invites the charge that research results and course content will be shaped by what the customer wants, rather than what evidence dictates. Yet Warwick has been an outstanding success, by academic and commercial measures.

The philosophically minded few and the pragmatical many have surprisingly little contact in academia, despite the relevance of theoretical concerns to important economic, political, psychological and sociological issues. It means that there are conflicting perspectives on the same human concerns, providing valuable if disputed insights into the way we live together and ways of improving it. As previously shown, the lack of discipline that spans specialisms can also lead to a trail of unfortunate applications. A variety of often conflicting models secures ubiquity but at a cost to validity, as the knowledge generated by discipline in specialist peer groups is compounded across their boundaries and filters down to those who seek its practical application.

Commerce Goes to College

Insiders' distaste at higher education being treated as, or run like, a business is fully understandable. On most dimensions, academic and commercial best practice are at opposite extremes. While businesses are urged to find and stick to a 'core competence', leaving other competences to strategic partners or subcontractors, universities try to contain contrasting subject competences. The mantra that teaching and research are mutually enhancing is maintained even as the two pull apart in terms of people, places and purse-strings, with professors scrambling to offload their lecturing to clear time for the next book or lecture tour. While businesses use improved information flow to focus on ever more tightly defined, synergistic customer segments, universities spread their net ever more widely: pitching research and teaching output at very different client groups, and adding a third 'wealth creation' mission whose output is imprecise and which takes the whole society as target beneficiaries.

Businesses link 'information age' success with achieving free flow of knowledge within themselves (to let every employee take well-intentioned initiatives and well-informed decisions), while rigidly containing internally generated knowledge within their boundaries (to stop rivals capturing proprietary secrets). Universities, in contrast, restrict their internal knowledge sharing through strict disciplinary boundaries and their deliberately differentiated languages, while encouraging free external sharing of knowledge, through exchanges of views and materials between counterparts at different institutions. Businesses acknowledge ever greater pressure to be 'customer driven', supplying what people want and catering to the growing immediacy and idiosyncrasy of their needs. Universities, conversely, pride themselves in being driven by supply side — delivering what is theoretically coherent and empirically supportable, and what people need to know, unmoved by what they might prefer to hear.

Perhaps most dramatically, businesses recognise that radical change often comes from outside established practices. New products and processes tend to be the work of new entrants, daring to think along lines the incumbents either failed to see or preferred to ignore because of investment in known ways of doing things. From Mars to Microsoft, companies that launch with one radical innovation rarely manage another of the same magnitude, despite being able to pour profits from the first into research towards the next. They survive, if at all, by structuring for rapid imitation of the next big breakthrough, or seeking it through 'intrapreneurial' units far removed from established operations. Universities, conversely, work to keep innovation an internal process, discounting radically different visions by excluding maverick inventors from the systems of refereeing and appraisal. While commerce celebrates the 'creative destruction' that consigns past bestsellers to the design museum, academe enshrines the defence of an archive that makes book-burning the cardinal sin.

The Academic 'Value Chain'

Knowledge has entered the industrial (and post-industrial) production system. But with equal force, the production system has entered knowledge. As its stock accumulates, opportunities arise for academics in relating, comparing, elaborating and applying knowledge, as well as creating more of it. Specialisation multiplies the opportunity to recombine and paraphrase knowledge for professional and general audiences.

Original knowledge is wholesaled by teaching-based universities, retailed by schools and specialist training institutions, repackaged by publishers and broadcasters for various sizes of wider audience, used as an input by businesses who resell it (and public agencies that assign it) as part of a 'value-added' output, and related or reinterpreted in the thoughts and conversations of ordinary citizens at the receiving ends of these chains. Precision in the production and laboratory testing of theory soon gives way to pick-and-mix, as priority shifts to professional applications and everyday use. As knowledge is compounded, validity can be lost through detachment of the application from the original inspiration.

As knowledge chains lengthen they grow increasingly tangled, as knowledge is compounded from discrete sources. Recombinations and reinterpretations, once established as a distinct subdiscipline, gain protection from the academic code of minding one's own validation business, however much they may offend those who produced the original components. The exercise of quality control is increasingly within small and narrow specialisms, often globally located. Each, however small, is linked electronically, publishes internationally, and expects its boundaries to be respected.

Compounding can be a particular problem for social scientists, who study a world interpreted through concepts they have produced. New theories change the construction. They also change the way human subjects are seen to understand. The facts collected through modelling, experimentation, observation and questioning are dependent on the assumptions behind the theories. It is safest to assume that all social scientific facts are theory-laden, resting on specific assumptions about ways of knowing, deterministic or interpretive, scientistic or hermeneutic. Eclecticism is dangerous because it is itself an assumption that reconciliation of theories and facts is unproblematic (Slife and Williams, 1995).

There is also a danger of premature or politically loaded application. This is greatest in applied, multidisciplinary and modular courses where incompatible, contradictory models are likely to be merged. Such courses were recommended in both the Robbins (1963) and Dearing (1997) reports on higher education, to secure the broad education wanted by students and employers. But a pick-and-mix approach can leave students struggling to find links between modules and chains of academic knowledge and the real world. For example, Organizational Behaviour (OB) draws on economics, psychology, sociology, social psychology, political science, social administration and industrial relations, with practical work in personnel psychology, organizational development, vocational and career counselling, vocational choice, personnel selection, performance appraisal and decision theory (Furnham 1997: 1–18). Multidisciplinary courses with vocational objectives stretch the original ideas so thinly, they may cease to show.

The distance from basic to applied, from those who produce to those who wholesale, retail and apply knowledge, further complicates the relation between knowledge users and producers. The currency trader rarely cares about the latest advances in econometrics. The social work tutor may know little of contemporary developments in social psychology. Aircraft makers initially knew little of the theory and experiment on metal fatigue. They may be forced to update when exchange rates plunge, a child's test scores plunge due to psychological bullying, or a Comet falls out of the sky.

Producers, wholesalers, retailers and popularisers of knowledge use different criteria in validation. Science and arts faculties view themselves as engaging with different worlds, and within each subject there are varied methodologies. Social scientists use methods that range from participant to structured observation through to controlled experimentation. Keeping these diverse activities coordinated, to ensure they complement each other and present a unified voice to the outside world, is the multiversity's first control task. With internal discipline established, it can move on to the second task: influencing the modification and application of knowledge beyond the sites at which it is originally produced.

Across academia it is a long way from discipline-grounded, basic theory to professional preparation. A little theory and a lot of illustrations can go a long way in presenting policies, explaining behaviour, advising professionals or getting on with the neighbours. Yet application without reference to the limitations imposed by basic assumptions in the assembly of knowledge of the social can harm just those they were intended to help. Crude and callous treatment of children was justified by reference to early behaviourist psychology. The sociological analysis of knowledge as class-based led to recommendations that children of the poor should not be pressured to learn literacy. Stalin justified mass murder by reference to Marx.

Popularisers, seeking to bridge the gap between academic specialists and general readers, must also link ideas and blend lines of reasoning in order to broaden the vision and deepen the understanding. The first popularisers were journalists or generalists who had swapped deep knowledge of one subject for an overview of many. A major extension of academics' control over ideas occurred when leading names moved from knowledge production into popularisation. Bookshop science shelves now sag under the intellectual weight of professors including Hawking (cosmology), Penrose (physics), Dawkins (biology) and Stewart (mathematics). Social science counterparts from sociologist Anthony Giddens to economist Gregory Mankiw have successfully attacked the textbook market.

This is partly a consequence of knowledge growing ever more abstruse, until only those near the cutting edge can convey what is now in their minds. It also reflects top researchers' acquiring capacity to broadcast or write, and being encouraged to do so by the rewards of outreach to a multiplying student population. But other motives challenge the view of academics' push into popularisation as producers' recapture of wholesale and retail applications. Catching the public imagination is a way of forcing peer recognition, especially when big ideas can be on the screen or front page months before the supporting academic papers find journal space. Sometimes maverick messages from James Lovelock, Stephen Jay Gould and Stephen Wolfram in the natural sciences, or Kenneth Galbraith, Hans Eysenck and Frank Furedi in the social, are moved closer to the mainstream by their circulation in quantity ahead of any academic consensus on their quality.

Social sciences' relaxed discipline of idealist, phenomenological, hermeneutic, interpretive and realist approaches accelerated the proliferation of applications, and the identification of new problems and solutions. There are now, for example, Sociological, Humanistic, Critical, Existential, Experiential and Experimental variants of Social Psychology, each further elaborated in the numerous Social Psychology of . . . courses given to trainee managers, social workers, teachers and others. Few who undertake these pay much attention to the ontological, epistemological and methodological concerns of those who first produced the ideas and evidence. By the time professionals and laity are influenced, several layers of caution may have been ignored.

The problems as value chains are stretched across academia from pure to applied, and as knowledge is compounded from different eras, are further exacerbated by knowledge being used across national and cultural boundaries. Academia may have become a global business, but there remain distinctive traditions in knowledge production. German academics have tended to draw a clear line between natural and social science. A German tradition drawing clear methodological distinctions between social and natural science collides with American and British scientist methods, but translation (mostly into English) facilitates their mixture. 'Austrian' market economics is often bracketed with the American 'neoclassical' variety, despite having roots in a radically different view of individuals and their choices. German gestalt psychology, focused on holistic thinking, intertwines uncomfortably with British and American reductionist behaviourism.

These contrasting national approaches are replicated in regional, racial, social class and gender influences on the social sciences. They may be written 'sans frontieres', but cultural differences can influence even the controlled experiment involving humans. Although the top ones circulate worldwide, listed references in academic journal articles or books are often overwhelmingly American. In the best-known European social psychology text in the mid-1990s, only a quarter of 2,000 citations were from outside North America (Smith and Bond, 1988: 3). Yet behavioural contingency management, self-fulfilling hypotheses or hierarchies of needs, developed through experiments involving American students, have no guaranteed relevance elsewhere (Furnham, 1997).

Cross-cultural studies tend to confirm that there are few if any universals in human thought and behaviour. A study of over 100,000 adults in 40 countries identified very broad differences between national cultures, despite their subjection to the unified 'corporate culture' of their employer IBM (Hofstede, 1980). Europeans and North Americans registered as high on individualism but low on 'power distance', the deference shown to those of different rank. In Latin America and Asia, individualism was low and 'power distance' high. These are significant factors in determining economic and social behaviour, as well as responses to social scientific enquiry. Psychometric tests measure personal characteristics according to 'norms' which differ across cultures, so tests imported to Europe from America have to be adjusted, for example, for Americans' systematically higher degree of extraversion. So the compounding of knowledge across nations and cultures adds to the complexity of academic value chains.

Detachment of observers from what they study, essential for validity in the work of natural scientists, is likely to undermine it in the work of social scientists because of their reflexive relation towards the subject. Easy electronic communication and the multiplication of journals has made cross-cultural referencing easier. The consequence has been the dominance of Western models of the world (Said, 1978; Geertz, 1993). But it is in the application of knowledge that most harm can be done, for here it can be compounded and stretched regardless of the often conflicting assumptions in its production. Small tweaks, particularly at the theoretical end of value chains, can be ignored or magnified as the knowledge moves through into applications, which have been the major area of expansion, especially in the social sciences.

Integrating the 'Knowledge Chain'

In business, the multiplication of intermediate steps between first producer and final consumer has placed a premium on 'supply chain integration'. Knowledge production encounters the same pressure once sped up by specialism. Between origination and application, theoreticians' insights must be tested, integrated with others to provide a bigger picture, translated into more accessible language and converted into a more readily absorbable format. Profit devolves towards whichever enterprise exerts — from within the chain or beyond it — coordinating power over the stages of production. Proliferation of producers at each stage increasingly means that the items passing down the chain are commodified, their price dropping close to their cost of production. Scarcity of chain integrators able to encompass the stages leaves them increasingly able to dictate the prices, quantities, qualities and times at which products flow between them.

Supermarket chains have become exemplars of chain integration from the final-demand end. By aggregating consumer demand they eliminate independent wholesalers, dictate terms to original suppliers, seize on marketable innovations while avoiding the risks of their development, and capture profit by setting costs and prices all along the chain. Car makers were, until recently, an exemplar of chain-integration from the original production end. Their concentration of supply allowed them to control the distribution network, setting sales outlets' prices and special offers to limit competition.

In industries where all stages are competitive, from original supply to final distribution, advantage is increasingly seized by 'virtual' integrators, who control the whole length of the supply chain without needing to own any part of it. In electronics, textiles, construction, power supply, abandoning direct involvement in any one production stage often assists towards the integration of the whole. Relieved of having to sink large investment into any specific production or service process, virtual integrators add value by assembling and coordinating all the relevant processes, leaving their delivery to specialist suppliers. Supermarkets' divestment of food production, and carmakers' outsourcing of design and sales, helped consolidate their overall control. Vertical integration — the enclosure of two or more supply chain stages within one organisation — has become rarer as lower transaction costs and more competitive markets make it easier to buy inputs in than to make them internally.

Universities have emerged as unrivalled integrators of the supply chain that underlies all others — that for knowledge itself. Against the commercial trend, which is for those closest to the consumer to extend control up the production chain, universities have achieved a producer-led integration, extending their control down the chain. As in the private sector, they have done so with an unusually low level of vertical integration. Ostensibly, the academy confines itself to higher education and original research. Downstream delivery of teaching was traditionally left to further education colleges and schools, and 'downstream' applications of research to industry, government and the professions. But universities have extended down the knowledge production chain, basing most of their recent growth on applications of knowledge, or repackaging it for wider consumption. While aspiring to theory and analysis, most academics spend most of their time testing, calibrating, relating and retailing ideas that already exist.

Academics consequently risk losing control of the knowledge they produce even within the university grounds. Only a few are isolated from pressures to produce knowledge that is useful to others. The elasticity of basic knowledge is a strength when used to reflect on practice in courses as diverse as Commerce, Exercise Studies or Social Welfare. Many multiversities have now dispensed with the specialist subject departments whose task was to produce the basic ideas and equip future specialists in these areas. But the reduction of downstream control is the cost of academic specialisation. Research-based universities have become the knowledge society's 'original equipment manufacturers'. But even at this first stage in the chain, there are challenges from commercial rivals offering cheaper lookalike qualifications, and vying for intellectual property rights. But whereas the company exists for, and aims to profit from, the private exploitation of knowledge, the academy's grounding in public knowledge gives it a very different reaction to the problem of control.

Knowledge-based firms invest heavily in certification and litigation to stop unapproved use of their products, or reputational damage from inferior imitations. Some academics have always worried about misuse of their wisdom in its downstream application, and expressed annoyance at the large cohort of colleagues who fail to share their concern. For every physicist who campaigns against military use of nuclear technology, and materials scientist who fears for ferroconcrete on housing estates, there are many who view politicians' and professionals' use of their work as beyond their control and concern. Even when their research is commercially or politically sponsored, many argue that they are merely revealing neutral truths about the planet and its people. Subsequent conversion of their new chemical into a defoliant, or new trade theorem into a reason to block Chinese imports, is held to reflect the social and moral climate around them and not their own integrity.

Increasing conceptual and presentational complexity of knowledge widens the gap between origination and application, making it easier to claim that research is merely revealing neutral truths, whose application to people and the planet is someone else's concern. But such an opt-out underplays academia's influence beyond its walls. The world around us has come to be understood through academic concepts, models and theories. These influence everyday thoughts and reactions when thinking of borrowing money, feeling unloved, switching detergent brand or worrying about crime. They also influence the majority of wholesaling and retailing academics, whose qualification for the job depends on accepting and relaying those models.

Nowhere is that more important than in studies that intersect with human thought and behaviour. Natural science has now been refined into theories and evidence that only specialists can fully understand, and which others' common sense and causal observation can do little to challenge. But social scientists, even a long way down the academic value chain, redefine the human condition and suggest solutions to the problems they identify. Authority ensures an impact from the Oxbridge don contemplating the social animal, but availability can mean equal impact for the lecturer explaining the significance of ethnomethodology to trainee nurses. Outside academia, the management guru and agony aunt draw on social science, albeit selectively, to advise on the decreasing number of issues still not fully absorbed within academic walls.

Like their commercial counterparts, wholesalers and retailers of knowledge can 'add value' to the original by compounding and applying it, making the insights more intelligible and useful, and often exploiting 'synergies' between areas that those absorbed in one of them are slow or unable to recognise. That is why popularisers from outside academia, blending to promote understanding, benefit from bridging the widening gap between academic specialists and an expanding lay audience that needs to keep track of expert opinion. Despite academics' inroads into the bookshops and broadcasting networks, public perceptions of social and natural science remains heavily shaped by media-friendly voices that stayed only briefly at university before leaving or transcending it. George Soros on economics and finance, Edward de Bono on psychology, Anthony Sampson on politics, David Starkey on history and Bill Gates on computing are among those filling lucrative gaps between 'pure' origination and popularisation.

The distance between production, wholesaling and retailing of knowledge increases intellectually as its originators rise to higher conceptual and conversational planes, while its disseminators and popularisers reach out to more mundane audiences. Distance also increases spatially as research institutes and centres for advanced study seek locations further removed from the training centres and technology colleges. There is less necessity for temporal distance to increase. Indeed, faster communication should enable those assimilating and applying knowledge to update themselves faster on the newest discoveries and interpretations of those digging at its coalface. Industrial value chains have become increasingly 'concurrent' as their integrators accelerate the transmission of customer orders up the line into production, and the diffusion of product development innovations down the line into marketing and sales.

However, lengthening of academic value chains has increased the scope for their stages to move out of phase. There can be long assimilation lags, with wholesalers and retailers peddling a once conventional view long after its originators have changed their minds or been replaced. Bohr's planetary model of the atom, Maslow's hierarchy of needs and Marshall's self-equilibrating macroeconomy remained popular in the classroom long after being superseded in the staffroom. There can also be time when knowledge's distributors get ahead of its creators, especially when a new idea captures the public imagination before it has completed the often slow process of formal validation. Einstein's ideas on curved space, Darwin's on evolution and Lucas's on rational expectations had edged onto many colleges' curricula long before supporting evidence was sufficient to secure general academic endorsement.

Pressure for External Regulation

The expansion of applied, modular and professional courses in the modern multiversity complicates the academic judgement of standards achieved. How are the many assessments from discrete modular courses to be weighted? How can the standard of courses compounded from many different specialisms be judged? What if success as a teacher in the classroom is not matched by performance on a concurrent Education course? Academics' upstream specialisation makes compounding inevitable. Those teaching modular courses must mix insights from many disciplines with those drawn from popular culture, the arts and the real world. Assessing validity involves a wide range of criteria from diverse reference groups. There is a growing likelihood of external criticism, especially of social science, whose success exposes it to the scepticism of an educated population expecting experts to have answers they can implement and understand.

The problems reported in Chapter 6 as academics and practitioners apply knowledge of limited reliability and validity are exacerbated by popularisation. Measured by sales and public acceptance, centuries of painstaking scholarship would quickly be eclipsed by Erich von Daniken's brand of science and Dan Brownian theology. Although the academy now sits proudly at the top of a lengthy intellectual supply chain, the lower reaches are ignored. However, the critical scrutiny of academic peers can also be relaxed. Peers in the same specialist team can take an overly benign view of each other's work, even as competitors take an overly malign view. The system of tenure was designed to ensure that scholars could retain their posts even if their written and spoken output [or lack of it] was judged negatively for long periods. While peer pressure is portrayed as the ultimate 'contest system', those working under it still do so with fundamental 'sponsored system' protections that have been reduced but not removed.

Academics tend to assume the reliability of insiders and focus their critical energy on those outside their peer group. So they quickly shoot down misleading results from people not expected to find them, like Velikovsky's curious cosmology and Pons and Fleischman's cold fusion. But they have been slow to challenge the

equally outrageous claims of the eminent, such as Cyril Burt's multiplying twin studies, or the Samoan confirmations of Franz Boas's
views on cultural variation by his student Margaret Mead. Where
there has been premature application, as in the cases reported in
Chapter 6, external concern is inevitable. The professions, usually
represented on the councils of universities, insist on a say over the
balance of theory and practice in training. The increasing academic
involvement in research for industry and government brings with it
constraints over what is produced and published. From the 1970s
on, government-appointed councils increasingly dictated the content of teacher and social work education, and insisted on inspection in academia to check that directions were being followed. By
the end of the 1990s the Central Council for the Education and
Training of Social Workers and the Teacher Training Agency were
establishing national curricula for academia to follow. University
autonomy shrunk with expansion.

Excluding Oxford and Cambridge, the constitution of most universities includes court, council, senate and faculty boards, all primarily concerned with the reconciliation of the academic, the
administrative and demands from government, professions and
other external bodies. All will have sub-committees reporting to
them. Court is a large body including representatives of diverse
interests, local, national and academic. Council takes responsibility
for finance and considers proposals from senate, which, usually
chaired by the vice-chancellor, decides on academic concerns.
Much of the business of senate comes from faculty boards which
deal with curriculum, teaching, research and examinations. Sena-
tors are a mix of professors and other academics representing the
interests of subjects, schools or faculties.

Professions also have codes of conduct and central watchdogs to
try to maintain standards. The academy's professional rule book is
necessarily thin, because of the many often murky ways to create
and convey great thoughts. So when the accounting, financial service, schoolteaching, medical and even legal professions were
brought under closer public monitoring, as a result of late twentieth
century scandals, the tide towards external regulation of academia
became hard to resist. Professions' entry regulation, while
explained by the need to keep up standards, can also be viewed as
an expedient to keep the supply of practitioners down and their
market price up, adding to the temptation to 'democratise' knowledge by breaking down academics' exclusive right to supply and
apply it.

Despite the difficulty of defining procedural rules, academics have where possible formed their own professional associations. Membership signifies that technical standards have been met and ethical standards respected. The associations can claim to speak for their subject, and are consulted by government. Their in-house journals become the official channels for professional discovery and opinion. The British Psychological Society (BPS), established in 1901 by those wishing to distinguish their 'scientific' approach to mental study and therapy from the many bogus practitioners, lays down conditions for recognising courses and the qualifications that form the criteria for membership. It still actively regulates out-of-house applications of psychological research, for example assessing and approving the many 'psychometric tests' now used in industrial and public service recruitment. Up to 1988, membership secured the right to practice under BPS auspices. Since then the BPS has established a register of chartered psychologists, requiring a recognised qualification, completion of a further training course, BPS approval of fitness to practice, and a promise to abide by the BPS code of practice and decisions of its disciplinary committee.

Absence of direct therapeutic or commercial applications does not prevent academics establishing professional accreditation. The British Sociological Association (BSA) was established in 1952, replacing the motley collection of historians, philosophers, journalists, politicians and clergymen, town planners, geographers and businessmen that had formed the Sociological Society in 1903. Both the BPS and BSA enjoyed the energies of Galton in their original foundation, and both were initially involved in the eugenics movement. The BSA took inspiration from its American counterpart, launched in 1905. By the 1960s, as numbers of young specialist sociologists multiplied, attempts were made to limit full BSA membership to those formally qualified. As this would have meant excluding many professors already in post, the distinguishing title 'fellow' was suggested. In 1961 a Teachers' Section was established with a series of 'gates' through which qualified applicants could pass. However, this attempt was also abandoned as the number of sociologists in technical and teacher training colleges increased.

As the BSA experience suggests, the desire to professionalise arose at least in part from fears that academics would lose status (and salary) as their numbers expanded. By showing they could set and implement their own standards, for long-established academic subjects as well as the more recently incorporated professional ones, universities hoped to replicate the respectability and autonomy already attained by self-regulating professional groups. However, the drive to emulate the professions gathered pace just as their self-regulatory privilege was starting to erode. The golden egg had hatched into a Trojan horse, exposing universities — and the knowledge-based activities they had academised — to growing pressures for external regulation.

As preparation of an increasing range of professions moved to the centre of their activities, the universities were faced with a dilemma. The traditional emphasis, traceable to Cardinal Newman's *The Idea of a University* (1858), is on preserving knowledge as an end in itself. The modern reinterpretation summarised by the Dearing Report (1997), is on producing knowledge and knowers to benefit the economy. With most academics working in vocational courses, reference is widened to professional, industrial and political interests as well as academic peers. Freedom can easily be compromised in the quest for students, funds and influence. Universities cannot claim their central place in the post-industrial, knowledge-based economy without succumbing to that economy's marketplace and regulatory pressures.

It is hard to disentangle academic ambition from the motivation to create new knowledge. While some rewards are intrinsic, many arise from career advance, publication opportunity, pioneering reputation and subject-leader status. Specialisation also offers a shield from competition, ruling out sudden invasion from other fields of knowledge. Subject-specific language, training and referencing put the specialist in a position to deny the legitimacy of criticisms by outsiders. But the claims of an expert elite to determine what counts as knowledge, and present it for unquestioning acceptance by the wider public, inevitably clash with demands for information on and involvement in the knowledge-creating process — from the public, and from governments that tax that public to pay for academia.

So from fending off threats posed by rival producers of knowledge, the academy has moved to confronting the challenge of dissatisfied consumers. Where apostasy, heresy and treason charges were Tudor scholars' main occupational hazard, contemporary threats lie in relations to government, industry and military, whose rising expenditure on university courses and research programmes gives them a similarly keen concern over the returns received. Since the state has become a major employer or paymaster of professional administrative, legal, medical, accounting and educational services, one motive for this attack was the financial one of breaking their restrictive hold on supply and pricing so that the cost of employing them could be controlled.

UK higher education has been described, not just by indignant free-marketeers, as the last great nationalised industry (Wolf 2002). A few prestigious institutions have reduced the state-funded proportion of their research budgets to little more than half, and discussed renouncing the rest of it. But private endowments, even of the ancient universities, remain a fraction of the size that lets top US universities finance themselves privately while still assigning places on merit rather than wealth. The UK's one private university, Buckingham, built its reputation only by accepting the public regulation of standards it originally sought to escape, and has not yet been flattered by any imitation.

Universities' dependence on funds from taxation puts governments under pressure to get value for public money. Even when it passes the tuition and maintenance bills on to students and their families, and asks private enterprise that benefits from university research to stump up more of the costs, the state perceives a duty to regulate standards. The Quality Assurance Agency (QAA), established in 1997, is intended to ensure that there is public confidence in higher education through visitations that result in audits of subject areas based on benchmarked standards. Regular Research Assessment Exercises (RAE), also based on inspection visits, result in formal rankings of departments and journals, and informal grading of those who work and publish in them. Many academics view their subjection to such assessments, and resultant league-table rankings, as part of the wider move to an 'Audit Society'. Audit has always been a part of academic life, but is part of a wider battle to preserve the academy's values against the organisational consequences of its growth.

Knowledge society may imply a guaranteed role for the multiversity and its expanding workforce. But this is no more certain than the survival of a modern corporation in the knowledge economy. Through their own efforts, social scientists have increased the demand for solutions while reducing the power and durability of those they supply. Audiences that once passively accepted the wisdom from pulpit and lectern are now educated to answer back. The market for academic knowledge is getting tougher.

Conclusion: Customer-Driven to Distraction

Monopolies have never been popular except with their owners. If governments sanction a sole supplier, it is because they are one of the profiting shareholders, or because the monopoly is seen as 'natural'. But economists retracted this category almost as quickly as

they advanced it, admitting that few industries have the scale economies that leave room for only one producer, and that governments
buying essential services on society's behalf can still take them from
a variety of sources. Industrial monopolies have been under attack
for more than a century, and professional monopolies are now similarly besieged. To defend their dual monopoly, on higher learning
and research, universities cite the damage inflicted on knowledge if
other agencies are given a role in its validation and dissemination.
They point out the greater trust enjoyed by universities — compared with government, industry or the church — in performing
these roles, based on their perceived pursuit of reliable knowledge
without a biasing agenda. And they point to the benign exercise of
the monopoly, keeping costs down so that courses are assigned by
merit not money, and making freely available knowledge for which
private producers would charge a price.

As positivism retrenches and postmodernism advances, the
struggle to keep control of knowledge widens into a struggle to control what counts as knowledge. Traditional criteria and procedures
come under challenge as those paying for universities' services, privately or publicly, feel more able to assert their own ideas on what is
useful and valid output. The multiversity must attract resources
and students in a competitive market, where bargaining power is
increasingly with the customers.

Commercial entrepreneurs get rich by uncovering and exploiting
an unmet demand, or satisfying existing demand in a better or
cheaper way. There was no mass demand for the family car, the
home computer, the hypermarket or the internet until risk-taking
visionaries chose to make them widely available. But having
opened up a new market, business innovators must still obtain from
outside the materials and energy to build and deliver a product, or
the human resources and communication infrastructures to deliver
a service.

Academic entrepreneurs can go one better, internally generating
new supply to go with the newly revealed demand. New knowledge is built from nothing more than the knowledge already in
stock, reinforced by new data or reworked with new analysis. As a
further significant advantage, academics address a demand for
knowledge that tends to expand as more is absorbed. Businesses,
except where supplying addictive substances, find people's desire
(and willingness to pay) dwindling as they acquire more of the
product, whose sales may plateau and even decline when there is
no further scope for promotional price-cuts and no new customer
segments to bring on board.

Successful companies use profits from selling existing products to existing clients to produce or acquire and launch new ones, expanding their market and customer share. The fastest of these virtuous circles transforms garage start-ups into global brand-names within the founders' lifetime. But growth carries risks — of expanding operations faster than the resources needed to manage them, making wrong technological turnings, taking on activities outside the area of expertise. Often the over-reaching hand can swiftly regain its magic touch. But sometimes the lithe specialist becomes an atrophied conglomerate, or the jack of all trades gets defeated by an ace in each one.

Successful countries, under similar pressure to grow, are at comparable risk of 'imperial overstretch'. An expanding economy widens their political influence, creating both scope and incentive to subordinate other nations. Extraterritorial strength is initially self-reinforcing, turning national power into 'superpower', with influence and interests disproportionate to size. But the superpower can be sidetracked into adventures abroad that cost more in security than they deliver in wealth or prestige, once subordinate nations and cultures start wrestling with the one that grew too much.

Universities have encountered the same expansionary hazards, despite their aversion to commercial or political empire building. They must contend with similar problems to those of production plants in the commercial world. Growth creates three particular areas of tension.

First, the generation and sharing of knowledge requires cooperation among scholars, but the race to new knowledge creates competition between them. This competitive-cooperative tension is imperfectly resolved by dividing the arena into ever more finely separated specialisms. Second, while universities are seen as authoritative sources of what to do and believe, they depend on democratic participation in the shaping of action and belief. This autocracy-democracy tension is imperfectly solved by recognising knowledge as reflexive, but still giving academic judgement a privileged role in its ratification. Third, while knowledge creators insist on discipline to ensure factual correctness, sound interpretation and appropriate application of knowledge, knowledge wholesalers and retailers prioritise dissemination, to ensure the fastest and widest application. Discipline-dissemination tension is generated and explosions of knowledge can cause collateral damage. Academia can no longer claim the privileges of an exclusive, marginal institution. A final question arises: when authority is legitimated by exclusivity, who takes responsibility across specialisms?

Chapter 8

Academia in the Open Society

This book has charted the success of higher education in supporting the emergence of societies based on knowledge, and of ways of understanding the change in ways of life within those societies. It has documented academia's decisive role in the rejection of belief in a world beyond human creation and comprehension. This achievement involved both absorbing the production of knowledge and transmitting it to an increasing proportion of the population. It was largely accomplished across the twentieth century, within institutions whose traditional or recently acquired exclusivity was their basis for ensuring the validity of that knowledge. Tension was inevitable.

Accelerating change across the twentieth century from cloister to multiversity was a challenge to the traditional authority of academics, exposing them to an increasingly competitive market for higher education. A university degree was initially a qualification to teach across universities. Now it is the basic entry qualification for skilled occupations, with increasing demand for the higher degree that distinguishes an increasing minority. Even the most McAdemised university, developed from a technical college or teacher training past, is more than a knowledge factory. The granting of university status, with its accompanying autonomy, has helped to spread the view of higher education as essential for realising the potential of individuals in a world where brain takes precedence over birth.

In Britain, the twentieth century began with extended schooling to secure mass literacy and numeracy. It ended with a majority being exposed to 'higher' education: not just to produce but to change production, not just to behave but to understand behaviour, not just to live with change but to manage and lead it. As public education was extended from infancy to adulthood, the natural and social sciences were inserted into the curriculum, challenging established beliefs. One author of this book was taught in an elementary school that Adam and Eve's unspecified but shady behaviour accounted for our sinful world. In secondary school we had evolved under the supervision of God. In university our reality was constructed through reason and interaction, and essay crises meant a trip to the library for extra reading rather than the chapel for extra prayer.

Academia's current problems arise from its success, and the specialisation that secures it. Any quality control across specialisms violates norms of peer validation within. Interference in the work of even closely related peer groups is taboo. Even those who analyse the problems of higher education scrupulously avoid examining the use made of theories and evidence as they pass along the value chain. Authority is vested with groups of mutually validating specialist peers. Yet the knowledge produced and validated is no longer exclusive but widely applied.

The social sciences have not just been rapidly organised as major parts of higher education, but are reflexive, and hence a test case of the relation between academics and the knowledge they provide in an educated society. They are engaged with their thinking subjects as they reinterpret past and present and predict futures. Natural scientists study a world that has evolved over some 14 billion years since a big bang. Social scientists not only face rapid social change, but help to produce it. Inevitably there is tension between the exclusivity that secures validity and the involvement necessary for application. These are reflexive sciences, ubiquitous and rewarding, but easily slipping into tautology as models are proliferated and elaborated.

The acknowledgement of this reflexivity, that social scientists both influence and are influenced by their human subjects, is a challenge to conventional scientific status. It has been beneficial in eliminating the scientistic arrogance that modelled humans on rats, tortured them to test reactions, justified policies such as genocide and eugenics and taught teachers and social workers that intelligence was fixed at birth. The widened contemporary range, from globalisation and international relations to love and eroticism, aimed at understanding rather than explanation, is in even more need of critical interpretation, not just by academics, but by those who apply their ideas and are affected by them.

There is, however, a problem in managing social scientific applications. Where reductive natural science can replicate rapidly and decisively, social science can be unfalsifiable. Pons and Fleischmann announced benchtop, room temperature nuclear fusion with four watts of output for every one of input on 23 March 1989. The US Department of Energy's Energy Research Advisory Board set up an expert panel to investigate on 13 April. An interim report on 12 July concluded there was no convincing evidence of a useful source of energy. The final report of 30 October confirmed that cold fusion had not been produced (Huizenga, 1992). In contrast, the shaping of behaviour by instincts was still being taught on teacher training courses fifty years after the long-forgotten McDougall had presented his original list.

Two recent reports have discussed the future for social science, the academy's first internally constructed discipline and the one that has driven its contemporary growth. Dahrendorf, an eminent European public servant, member of the Bundestag and Director of the LSE (1974–84) admits to producing two answers to the question *Whither Social Science?* (Dahrendorf, 1995b). One was full of doubts and uncertainties, confirming the difficulty when academic autonomy accompanies influence. The final published version avoided the question in the title, and concluded that academia could find a way through its problems by establishing institutes of advanced study that would produce knowledge for the sake of knowledge, thus avoiding the problem of its increased influence.

The Gulbenkian Commission on the Restructuring of the Social Sciences (1996) focused on the problems of exclusive specialisation. Hence its title, *Open the Social Sciences*. It recommends establishing research groups and post-graduate study focused on interdisciplinary and thematic topics, with the compulsory appointment of professors with interests spanning subject boundaries. This was never likely to break open specialisms secured by exclusive career paths, canon and language, each with its own definitions of the human. Social scientists are no longer a few pioneers choosing ways forward in open country. They are established in closed specialisms, with authority derived from exclusivity, and wary of recommendations that would challenge their legitimacy.

There are problems in any quality-control policy that challenges this specialist authority in higher education. Solutions currently on offer include separation into teaching and research institutions; adoption of a McAdemised profit-making business model with students supported through voucher schemes; letting academics conduct quality control of the whole process of producing, validating and applying knowledge; extending current external examination, course approval and research assessment by peers; continuing the move to becoming the third stage of popular education, with a fourth stage evolving for post-graduate study; or resisting any external attempts at reform that touch the production and transmission of knowledge. All are possibilities. But all disturb the peace of the cloister, by letting external political or market forces intrude.

It is the importance of academia that accounts for the increased concern. In the mid-nineteenth century Newman could stress the autonomy of the university and its concern with knowledge as an end in itself. Over a century later, the Robbins and Dearing Reports stressed its instrumental, economic importance. But to be useful, knowledge has to be comprehensible from producers to consumers. Academics secure their authority through peer validation and exclusive specialist discourses. In social science they have promoted the rationalisation of the modern world, but in a way that re-mystifies as well as de-mystifies. When the subject is the complex thinking human, application can result in catastrophes, some recalled in Chapter 7.

This tendency to add new mysteries while dispelling old ones, and take over sacked priestly and princely palaces, is consolidated by the differentiated structure of academia. As knowledge is passed from theory to application it is liable to be compounded, with other ideas based on incompatible assumptions. That is exacerbated by the lack of overall quality control. The rise of the Economics of, Psychology and, Sociology with, and various integrated studies has been followed by the launch of business, cultural, development, feminist, media, queer and other Studies. Each rapidly acquires global reach and specialist departments, publications, professional associations and language. This has been facilitated by the widespread granting of university status, with its accompanying autonomy.

The most obvious solution to the coexistence of exclusivity and application is for academics to accept responsibility for the quality and use of the knowledge they produce. That would also open up the university to the scrutiny of an increasingly educated society. It would be an acknowledgement of success, not an admission of failure. Educated populations should be in a position to assess the validity and reliability of the knowledge on which they depend. At present even graduates may not have the necessary critical capital. From the first contact with social science in schools to graduation, this ability to assess knowledge should be a priority, however uncomfortable this would be for its producers.

Scientific validity depends on knowledge being open to criticism (Popper 1959). No science has a firm bedrock, all rely on conjecture. Theories rest on piles driven into a swamp, firm enough for confidence but with no fundamental foundation, and always needing to be tested. The expansion of higher education means this testing can now be extended, not exclusive. Knowledge should be open to informed professional and lay assessment, recognising that those who put ideas into practice are often best placed to see their weaknesses and unexplored possibilities. That applies in particular to social scientific knowledge, where there are always cases that falsify, more so as the world undergoes change for which the knowledge is partly responsible. Knowledge of the human in society is produced outside as well as inside academia, by poets and playwrights as well as psychologists and sociologists, bankers and financial journalists as well as economists. While born in the academy, social science now ranges too widely to be confined to it.

Academisation poses an additional problem. As specialisms have been organised into professional associations, academics define and defend their specialist boundaries. Criticism from outsiders is resented. But academics are no longer an elite in an uneducated mass. If knowledge grows out of disagreement, not consensus, then today's settled career tracks, subject consensuses and harmonious systems of referencing impose an unproductive calm. The sources of scrutiny and review, dissent and criticism outside academia should be encouraged by those within, not excluded and resented. It is absurd to model the human as rational or thoughtful or constructive and then exclude them by academic deadpan.

The reluctance of academics, particularly social scientists, to recognise that they now inform an educated population has been a recurring theme of this book. Academia not only qualifies increasing numbers, but simultaneously raises expectations of knowing. With universal secondary schooling and approaching one half of students going on to higher education, social scientists study informed and thinking humans. To be exclusive is to seal academia off from its subject matter, to invent an unthinking social animal, to repeat the Enlightenment view of the majority as canaille.

A transition to an open intellectual environment would involve changes within academia, in its relations with the 'periversity' of professionals, industry, politicians and the public. Academics would have to take responsibility for ensuring that their assumptions are explicit, the logic of their methods clear, their evidence reliable, their language comprehensible beyond their peers. Above all, there would be openness in assessing validity. Such transparency would mean a loss of authority. The gain would be in raising public understanding of the academy's scope and limits, especially in social science, and so replacing the lost respect for the academic based on eminence to a new one based on evidence. Of all the enterprises of the Enlightenment, academia should have avoided the arcane, and accepted its fallibility (Popper, 1994: 185–209). Nowhere is that more important than in the reflexive sciences now seeking to serve, and draw support from, the educated society.

References

Argyris C. & Schon D. (1978) *Organizational Learning*, Reading, Mass: Addison-Wesley

Becher T. (1989) *Academic Tribes and Territories*, Buckingham: Open University Press.

Bernal J.D. (1939) *The Social Function of Science.* London: Routledge.

Bernstein B. (1970) A critique of the concept of compensatory education, in Rubinstein D. and Stoneman C. (eds.), *Education for Democracy*, Harmondsworth: Penguin, pp. 110–126.

Bernstein B. (1996) *Pedagogy, Symbolic Control and Polity: Theory, research, critique*, London: Taylor and Francis.

Bloom H. (1999) *Shakespeare: The invention of the human*, London: Fourth Estate.

Bowles S. & Gintis H. (1976) *Schooling in Capitalist America* New York: Basic Books

Bowles S. & Gintis H. (1986) *Democracy and Capitalism*, London: Routledge and Kegan Paul.

Clawson D. (1998) *Required Reading: Sociology's most influential books*, Amherst: University of Massachusetts Press.

Dahrendorf R. (1995a) *The London School of Economics*, Oxford: Oxford University Press.

Dahrendorf R. (1995b) *Whither Social Sciences?* Swindon: Economic and Social Research Council.

Dasgupta P. & David P. (1988) Priority, secrecy, patents and the socio-economics of science and technology, Center for Economic Policy Research report 127, Stanford University.

Dawkins R. (1989) *The Selfish Gene*, 2/e Oxford: Oxford University Press.

Delanty G. (2001) *Challenging Knowledge: The University in the Knowledge Society*, Buckingham: Society for Research into Higher Education & Open University Press.

Doman G., Doman J. and Aisen S. (1994) *How to Teach your Baby Encyclopedic Knowledge*, New York: Avery

Duverger M. (1964), *Introduction to the Social Sciences*, London: Allen and Unwin, p.73.

Elashoff J.D. & Snow, R.E. (1971) *Pygmalion Reconsidered*, New York: Jones.

Esland G.M. (1971) Teaching and Learning as the Organization of Knowledge, in Young, M.F.D., *Knowledge and Control*, Collier Macmillan, pp. 70–115.

Evans M. (2004) *Killing Thinking: The death of the universities*, London: Continuum.

Foucault M. (1972) *The Archeology of Knowledge*, New York: Pantheon.

Furnham A.F. (1997) *All in the Mind*, London: Whurr.

Geertz C. (1993) *Local Knowledge*, London: Fontana.

Goffman E. (1961) *Asylums*, New York: Anchor.

Habermas J. (1972) *Knowledge and Human Interests.* London: Heinemann.

Hare N. (1985) *Controversies in Teaching*, Brighton: Wheatsheaf.

Harre R. (1993) *Social Being*, Oxford: Blackwell.

Hayek F.A. (1974) The Pretence of Knowledge (Nobel Memorial Lecture, Stockholm, 11 December 1974), *New Studies in Philosophy, Politics, Economics and the History of Ideas*, London: Routledge and Kegan Paul.

Hesse M. (1980) *The Structure of Scientific Information*, London: Macmillan.

Hofstede G. (1980) *Culture's Consequences: International differences in work-related values*, Beverly Hills, CA: Sage.

Holt J. (1965a) *How Children Fail*, New York: Pitman

Holt J. (1965b) *How Children Learn*, New York: Pitman

Huizenga J.R. (1992) *Cold Fusion: The scientific fiasco of the century*. Oxford: Oxford University Press.

Kerr C. (1963) *The Uses of the University*, New York: Harper & Row.

Knorr-Cetina K.D. (1982), *The Manufacture of Knowledge*, Oxford: Pergamon.

Kuhn T. (1962) *The Structure of Scientific Revolutions*, Chicago: University of Chicago Press.

Lakatos I. (1978) *Collected papers*, Cambridge: Cambridge University Press.

Laudan L. (1977) *Progress and its problems:toweards a theory of scientific growth*, London: Routledge.

O'Neill O. (2002) *A Question of Trust*, Cambridge: Cambridge Univ. Press.

Peters D.P. and Ceci, S.J. (1982) Peer Review Practices of Psychological Journals, in Harnad, S. (ed) (1982) *Peer Commentary on Peer Review*. Cambridge: Cambridge University Press.

Popper K.R. (1959) *The Logic of Scientific Discovery*, London: Hutchinson.

Popper K. R. (1994) *The Myth of the Framework*, London: Routledge.

Price G. (1966) 'Education as a main course', *Education for Teaching*, 70, pp. 4–12.

Ritzer G. (2000) *The McDonaldization of Society*, Thousand Oaks: Pine Forge Press.

Rosenthal R. & Jacobsen L. (1968) *Pygmalion in the Classroom*, New York: Holt Rinehart and Winston

Said E. (1978) *Orientalism*, London: Routledge and Kegan Paul.

Slife B.D. and Williams, R.N. (1995) *What's Behind the Research? Discovering hidden assumptions in the behavioural sciences*, London: Sage.

Smith P.B. and Bond M.H. (1988) *Social Psychology Across Cultures*, London: Prentice-Hall.

Starbuck W. (2003) 'Turning lemons into lemonade: where is the value in peer reviews?' *Journal of Management Inquiry*, 12(4), 344–351.

Stone M. (1981) *The Education of the Black Child in Britain*, London: Fontana.

Thompson E.P. (ed) (1971) *Warwick University Ltd*, London: Penguin

Tischmann J., Dennis A., Northcraft G. & Nieni A. (2000), 'Serving multiple constituencies in business schools: program vs research performance', *Academy of Management Journal*, 43, 1130–41

Wenneras C. and Wold A. (1997) Nepotism and sexism in peer review, *Nature*, 22 May, 377, pp. 341–343.

Whitley R. (2000) *The Intellectual and Social Organization of the Sciences*, 2/e, Oxford: Oxford University Press

Wolf A. (2002) *Does Education Matter?* London: Penguin

Wood F.Q., Meek, V.L. and Harman, G. (1992) The research grant application process: learning from failure. *Higher Education*, 24, pp.1–23.

Wootton B. (1959) *Social Science and Social Pathology*, London: Allen Unwin.

Index

SOCIETAS: essays in political and cultural criticism

Public debate has been impoverished by two competing trends. On the one hand the trivialization of the media means that in-depth commentary has given way to the ten second soundbite. On the other hand the explosion of knowledge has increased specialization, and academic discourse is no longer comprehensible. As a result writing on politics and culture is either superficial or baffling.

This was not always so — especially for political debate. The high point of the English political pamphlet was the seventeenth century, when a number of small printer-publishers responded to the political ferment of the age with an outpouring of widely-accessible pamphlets and tracts. But in recent years the tradition of the political pamphlet has declined—with most publishers rejecting anything under 100,000 words. The result is that many a good idea ends up drowning in a sea of verbosity. However the introduction of the digital press makes it possible to re-create a more exciting age of publishing. *Societas* authors are all experts in their own field, but the essays are for a general audience. Each book can be read in an evening. The books are available retail at the price of £8.95/$17.90 each, or on bi-monthly subscription for only £5/$10. Details/updated schedule at **imprint-academic.com/societas**

EDITORIAL ADVISORY BOARD

Prof. Jeremy Black (Exeter); Prof. Robert Grant (Glasgow); Prof. John Gray (LSE); Prof. Robert Hazell (UCL); Prof. Anthony O'Hear (Bradford); Prof. Nicholas Humphrey (LSE); Dr. Efraim Podoksik (Hebrew Univ., Jerusalem)

IMPRINT ACADEMIC, PO Box 200, Exeter, EX5 5YX, UK
Tel: (0)1392 841600   Fax: (0)1392 841478   sandra@imprint.co.uk

SOCIETAS SUBSCRIPTION FORM

All Societas titles are available at the reduced price of £5.00 each to subscribers. To qualify for the reduced price, simply sign up for the current volume by direct debit. We will debit your account £5.00 when each book is despatched (every two months). Details of the next title will be supplied at the same time, so if you want to unsubscribe you can cancel the mandate.

☐ *Please register my **Societas** subscription, starting with the current volume. I would also like to order the following backlist titles (first two at only £2.50 each, additional titles for £5.00)*

. . . .

. . . .

. . . .

. . . .

DIRECT Debit

IMPRINT ACADEMIC

Please fill in the form and send to Imprint Academic, PO Box 200, Exeter EX5 5YX

Instruction to your Bank or Building Society to pay by Direct Debit

To: The Manager — Bank/Building Society

Address

Postcode

Name(s) of Account Holder(s)

Branch Sort Code

Bank/Building Society account number

Originator's Identification Number

| 6 | 3 | 0 | 4 | 9 | 4 |

Reference

Instruction to your Bank or Building Society

Please pay Imprint Academic Direct Debits from the account detailed in this Instruction subject to the safeguards assured by the Direct Debit Guarantee. I understand that this instruction may remain with Imprint Academic and, if so, details will be passed electronically to my Bank/Building Society.

Signature(s)

Date

DDI5

Banks and Building Societies may not accept Direct Debit Instructions for some types of account

Name. . . . .

Address * . . . .

. . . .

Home telephone . . . . E-mail. . . . .

Send to: IMPRINT ACADEMIC, PO Box 200, Exeter EX5 5YX, UK
Tel: (0)1392 841600   Fax: (0)1392 841478   Email: sandra@imprint.co.uk